LIBERAL
THEOLOGY

Also by Peter C. Hodgson

Hegel and Christian Theology

The Mystery beneath the Real

Christian Faith

God's Wisdom

Winds of the Spirit

God in History

Revisioning the Church

New Birth of Freedom

Children of Freedom

Jesus—Word and Presence

The Formation of Historical Theology

LIBERAL
THEOLOGY

A
Radical
Vision

Peter
C.
Hodgson

Fortress Press
Minneapolis

LIBERAL THEOLOGY
A Radical Vision

Chapter 2 draws on material previously written about in *Hegel and Christian Theology* by Peter Hodgson (Oxford University Press, 2005), p. 259–284. Used by permission of Oxford University Press.

Cover photo © Neil Leslei/Digital Vision/Getty Images. Used by permission.
Cover design by Brad Norr Design
Book design by Douglas Schmitz

Library of Congress Cataloging-in-Publication Data
Hodgson, Peter Crafts, 1934-
  Liberal theology : a radical vision / Peter C. Hodgson.
    p. cm.
  Includes index.
  ISBN-13: 978-0-8006-3898-6 (alk. paper)
  1. Liberalism (Religion) 2. Theology, Doctrinal. I. Title.
  BR1615.H63 2007
  230'.046—dc22
                            2006103473

The paper used in this publication meets the minimum requirements of American National Standard for Information Sciences—Permanence of Paper for Printed Library Materials, ANSI Z329.48-1984.

Manufactured in the U.S.A.

11   10   09   08   07   1   2   3   4   5   6   7   8   9   10

For Eva

Once again, after all these years

Contents

Preface

THERE IS SOMETHING INTRINSICALLY RADICAL about theology. After all, it purports to make assertions about *God,* about the ultimate meaning and purpose of things, and it offers strong judgments about human behavior from a prophetic perspective. While drawing upon experience and history, its way of knowing and speaking brings into play revelation and intuition, story and poetry, philosophical speculation and religious faith. It is engaged with the real but seeks the mystery beneath the real. Karl Barth once remarked (quoting Franz Overbeck) that "theology can no longer be based on anything but daring." Could it ever be based on anything but daring?

Such daring drives theology to its roots, its *radix.* At the roots it discovers something remarkable: God's radical freedom, nature's incipient freedom, and humanity's liberated freedom. This, I believe, is the central message of liberal theology, whose very name coincides with its content, *libertas.* In this little book I call for a revival of liberal theology with a radical vision because I believe it offers deeper insight into the meaning and truth of Christian faith for today than all the other options. Liberalism has been under sustained attack for many years, and its dimunition or loss would have tragic consequences both politically and religiously. We would be left with the alternatives of fundamentalism and neoconservatism on one side, and atheism and secularism on the other—the reigning dogmatisms of our time. The great mediating matrix of theology would be destroyed. Liberal theology is capable of acknowledging its historical failings and of reinventing itself by taking up the work of mediation and freedom anew. Such at least is my thesis and my hope.

The first chapter, "A Radical Vision," introduces the idea of a radically liberal theology, positions it in relation to other options, identifies its marks, and explores its roots in the concept of God. The second chapter, "Contested Sites and Liberal Mediation," engages issues of philosophical theology and cultural analysis, draws upon a deep and daring thinker, G. W. F. Hegel, and offers hints for the reconstruction of central themes of Christian theology at points of fracture in postmodernity. The final chapter, "The Freedom Project," tracks the ethical implications of radical liberalism for emancipatory struggles, ecological awareness, interreligious dialogue, and contemporary politics.

Writing this book has provided an occasion for me to reflect on my own theological journey and to identify a legacy that seems worthy of passing on. Incorporated into these pages are materials from previous writings that I would like to make more accessible. I thank Ashgate Publishing, Orbis Books, Oxford University Press, and Westminster John Knox Press for permission to use these materials. I also thank Mary McClintock Fulkerson, Roger Haight, Christine Helmer, and Hyo-Dong Lee for reading the manuscript and offering helpful suggestions. The Consultation on Liberal Theologies invited me to present a paper at the meeting of the American Academy of Religion in November 2006; this paper became the germ of the present book, and without it the latter would not have been written. My first book in constructive theology was published by Fortress Press thirty-six years ago under the editorial auspices of Norman Hjelm, to whom I am indebted for helping to launch my vocation as a theologian; now I am grateful to Michael West for helping to bring it to completion.

Chapter 1

A
Radical
Vision

Postliberalism, Radical Orthodoxy, and Radical Liberalism

POSTMODERNITY POSES A COMPLEX SET of challenges to liberal theology. On the one hand, it calls into question many of the assumptions of modernity upon which liberalism is presumed to rest, assumptions about the primacy and universality of reason, the autonomy of the individual, the accomplishments of science and technology, the superiority of Western societies based on free-market capitalism, and so on. For postmodernity, old assumptions and stable structures have broken down. The complicity of modernity in systems of domination and control based on privilege, wealth, and power is clearly recognized, and the foundational narratives on which these systems were based and by which they were justified have collapsed.

They are being replaced by a perception of reality that is fluid, relative, permeable, something that is more like a net or a web than a building with foundations. Some of the elements of the postmodern sensibility, according to Paul Lakeland, are that it is nonsequential, noneschatological, nonutopian, nonsystematic, nonfoundational, and ultimately nonpolitical. Within all of these "nons" or negations, free play is given to a culture that is increasingly fragmented and oriented to the values of consumerism, sensual gratification, and gratuitous violence. The individual becomes a commodity in the play of conflicting forces—economic, political, and cultural. "The postmodern human being," writes Lakeland, "wants a lot but expects little. The emotional range is narrow, between mild depression at one end and a whimsical insouciance at the other."[1]

On the other hand, postmodernity offers some opportunities to theology. Elaine Graham writes, "The complexities of our situation are where liberal theology begins its work." Despite the instrumentalism and fragmentation with which she, too, is concerned, this work would involve looking also "to the qualities of the postmodern condition that might be of value: its fluidity, its pluralism and questioning of authority, its resistance to exclusivism and its openness to religious sensibilities characteristic of the postmodern return of the sacred."[2] The latter might offer some critical space for religion and some respite from the secular humanism that characterizes much of late modernity. We should be encouraged, she says, to address again some basic questions: What does it mean to be human? What kind of society do we want? And most important, What do we worship—gods and idols such as the state, the market, self-interest, progress? Or a God who radically transcends such idols but is also radically immanent in the world as the generative power of freedom?

Yes, liberal theology does its best work in the complexities of a situation. My argument in this book is that if and when liberal theology takes up its work again in the complexities of our present situation, it will find itself driven to its roots, the *radix*, and it will become a "radical liberalism." But should its work be taken up again? It has been relentlessly criticized as no longer relevant or even misleading and dangerous, starting with the revolution in theology instigated by Karl Barth and the neoorthodoxy of the dialectical theologians, continuing with various forms of evangelical and fundamentalist theology on the right, the death-of-God theologies and deconstructive "a/theologies" on the left, and finally the postliberal theology that arose in the 1980s and the radical orthodoxy of the 1990s and beyond. Ironically, during the past half-century creative theology in the liberal mode has continued to be produced in considerable abundance,[3] but it has been the work of a mostly older generation (my own) and the question now is whether it has run its course.

Barth himself studied under the leading liberal theologians of his time, but he became disillusioned when many of them signed a manifesto supporting the war policy of the German Kaiser in 1914.[4] He came to regard liberal theology as losing the radical claim of the gospel in an accommodation to the values of bourgeois culture. Late in his career, however, he spoke more appreciatively of the liberal tradition, describing himself as a "*truly* liberal theologian," and his own radical theology offers important resources for a radical liberalism, as I shall argue below.

Barth never engaged in the demonizing and scapegoating of liberalism that have become popular among conservative and fundamentalist critics, some of whom attribute to it all the evils of the modern world, including Stalinism and Nazism. He certainly did not share the standard caricature that liberal theology simply abandoned the foundations of Christian faith and rejected historical Christianity on the grounds that it is unacceptable to the modern mind.[5] He knew that liberal theologians were wrestling with difficult questions of interpretation that must be faced by every modern theology. These popular caricatures have been fueled partly by a backlash against black, third world, and feminist theologies, which offer a powerful critique of established social structures and prejudices, and by the profoundly conservative political turn in the United States, which defines liberalism as the enemy. Barth was strongly opposed to such reactionary views.

At the opposite extreme to fundamentalism are what Lakeland describes as the "radical postmoderns,"[6] who celebrate all the negations referred to earlier, are content to live without cultural orientation in a kind of aesthetic play of differences, are radically historicist (no self, no history, no book, no God, as Mark C. Taylor expresses it[7]), and regard knowledge to be purely a function of power, desire, and self-interest. These are the heirs of Friedrich Nietzsche, Michel Foucault, Jacques Derrida, and other deconstructive philosophers, as well as of the so-called death-of-God or radical theologies of the 1960s. From the point of view of this "a/theology," any attempt to continue to think theologically is doomed from the start. Here what are being radicalized are the cultural assumptions of postmodernity rather than, as I shall claim on behalf of liberal theology, the heart of the Christian gospel.

Between the two extremes of political-religious fundamentalism and radical postmodernism stand other theological options. While they share some basic critical assumptions, they are quite different and comprise a spectrum of the middle. At one end are what Lakeland calls the "countermoderns," for whom modernity itself is a problem (its liberalism, moral relativism, secular humanism, and so forth), and who celebrate its demise as an opportunity to reaffirm traditional truths and values, either by embracing a postcritical theory of knowledge and language, drawn especially from Ludwig Wittgenstein, which emphasizes the function of language in forming distinctive patterns of life, or by retrieving classical, premodern traditions in response to the negations of radical postmodernity. The two principal theological schools of countermodernity are postliberalism and radical orthodoxy. At the other end of the spectrum are the "late moderns" or "critical postmoderns," who live critically in the postmodern world, affirming some of it (the decentering of the human person, Western culture, and Christ), challenging other parts of it (its relativism, atheism, aestheticism), wanting to carry the unfinished project of modernity forward but in a vastly changed cultural world. Here various options have been explored, drawing upon pragmatism (William James, John Dewey, and their heirs), critical social theory (Jürgen Habermas), or a holistic philosophy of relationality and process (Georg Wilhelm Friedrich Hegel, Alfred North Whitehead).[8] The revisionary or radical liberalism I shall advocate is an example of the latter.

What are the issues at stake between postliberalism, radical orthodoxy, and radical liberalism?

1. Postliberal Theology

I recall, when I was a student at Yale Divinity School in the late 1950s, that H. Richard Niebuhr once identified himself as a "postliberal." By this term he intended to distance himself not only from a liberalism too oriented to human achievements but also from Barthian orthodoxy, which he feared would become a growing force following the death of the great theologian. He predicted that Barth's system would be absolutized by those on the right into a new orthodoxy and converted by those on the left into an anthropological subjectivism by reversing Barth's language.[9] In this he proved to be quite prescient. Thus, Niebuhr regarded himself as neither a traditional liberal nor a Barthian. He did not abandon liberalism but intended to appropriate it critically in light of valid criticisms. In lectures delivered at Vanderbilt Divinity School in 1961 (a year before his death), Niebuhr indicated that he was attempting to recover a balance between criticism of and appreciation for the great liberal theologians of the nineteenth century, as well as a balance between past and present, self and other, thought and action, objectivism and subjectivism, and, most importantly, the transcendence and immanence of God. By "balance" he did not mean a middle-of-the-road theology but a bold movement into the future and the forging of new symbols.[10] At the end of his career, clearly he believed that the neoorthodox reaction against liberal theology had gone too far and that a new balance was needed.

In the postliberal theology that arose at Yale two decades later, there was less concern for balance and more for identity, combined with an essentially critical rather than appreciative assessment of nineteenth-century liberalism. In the view of George Lindbeck, the principal problem of liberal theology is that it undermines the particularity and identity of Christianity by associating it with an "experiential-expressive" mode of religion that is common to all sincere searchers after wisdom. By attempting to mediate between the Christian message and the wider world, the specific content of this message is allowed to evaporate. Lindbeck's proposed alternative, the "cultural-linguistic" model, presents Christianity as a self-enclosed language game in which doctrines operate as grammatical rules. These rules set the limits of what Christians can say and believe, and it means that they must understand the world in their own terms. "It is the text . . . which absorbs the world, rather than the world the text." The "text" for Lindbeck is the narrative of Christian self-identity that is established by scripture and ecclesiastical confessions.[11] Not much in this proposed "postliberalism" is actually liberal, and from a Niebuhrian perspective it appears to be uncomfortably close to a new orthodoxy, even a kind of dogmatism. But it resonates with the postmodern suspicion of frameworks or metanarratives that purport to transcend specific cultures of discourse. We exist, so it is claimed, in a fragmented world of incommensurable differences.

The sort of postliberal position associated with another Yale theologian, Hans Frei, was shaped more by Barth, especially Barth's theological hermeneutics as related to biblical narrative and identity description, than by cultural theory.[12] Frei was thoroughly familiar with nineteenth-century Protestant liberal theology,[13] and his criticisms of it are more nuanced than those of Lindbeck. I was a student of Frei, as well as of Niebuhr and Lindbeck, and was deeply influenced by all of them. My studies occurred well before the time that postliberal theology had become a "school" associated with Yale.

One of Frei's and Lindbeck's most gifted students, Kathryn Tanner, while agreeing that theology is a culture-specific activity, argues that the notion of discrete cultural identity has been deconstructed by recent cultural theory. Cultures are in fact porous, interactive, and constantly evolving, so that cultural identity is a hybrid, relational affair. This means that while the identity of a Christian way of life is formed in relation to a cultural boundary, the latter is not a sharp boundary of independent cultural contents but a boundary that allows Christian identity to be impure and mixed, drawing upon various resources. The distinctiveness of the Christian way of life is formed not so much *by* the boundary as *at* it. However, this does not entail for Tanner a "correlation" with other cultural materials, as liberals might argue, but rather a construction of Christian identity by applying a qualifier or a "twist" to the materials. The twist, which seems to transcend cultural embeddedness, is provided by the Word of God revealed in Christ, and Christian identity depends on remaining open to direction from God's free grace in Christ.[14] Thus, Christ retains a primacy over culture, determining how its materials are to be appropriated in the construction of Christian identity; Christ is not so much a transformer *of* culture, passing *across* boundaries into other regions of human existence, shaping them and being shaped by them.[15] In this respect Tanner remains within the postliberal paradigm.

2. Radical Orthodoxy

Radical orthodoxy is more resolutely countermodern than postliberalism. It has been mostly a movement of high-church Anglicans and Catholics with a strong orientation to liturgical celebration as the context of theology and a critique of the logic of secularism, which it views as imploding upon itself, promoting a materialism that is soulless, aggressive, nonchalant, and nihilistic. In face of the secular demise of truth, radical orthodoxy seeks to reconfigure theological truth. A manifesto written by three of its leading advocates[16] announces that the movement is "orthodox" in the sense of being committed to creedal Christianity, especially in its patristic matrix, and to the medieval Catholic social order. It is "radical" in three senses: its return to patristic and medieval roots, especially to the Augustinian vision of all knowledge as divine illumination; its deployment of this vision to criticize modern society, culture, politics, art, science, and philosophy; and its reenvisioning of a Christianity that properly values the material, embodied sphere of life that alone can lead to God. It is a radicalism that refuses the secular by "suspending" it, replacing with a Platonic-Augustinian theory of "participation" that allows no territory independent of God and thus no "mediation" with an autonomous realm. Thus, every discipline must be framed by a theological perspective; there is simply (as Mark Chapman notes[17]) no true anything apart from God. Even Karl Barth failed to recognize this and was too accommodating—and too "ploddingly exegetical" by contrast with the "complex but coherently executed *collage*" of radical orthodoxy. Here a certain imperialism manifests itself in this new theology, reflected also in its claims on behalf of the superiority of Christian rationality, its privileging of Christianity vis-à-vis other religions, and its proposal of a "peaceable kingdom" that asphyxiates differences.[18]

One critic attempts to move radical orthodoxy in the direction of "liberal orthodoxy" or "rational liberalism." Michael Langford offers a defense of the tradition of Christian rationalism from the second to the seventeenth centuries.[19] He believes that we can adopt only part of the Enlightenment's trust in reason without becoming committed to an overly optimistic view. His preference is for a premodern rationalism that integrates rationality and faith and defends the reality status of God. Thus, he does not embrace the Protestant liberal theology of the nineteenth and twentieth centuries; his orientation is to a more traditional form of Anglicanism.

3. Radical Liberalism

When I retired in the spring of 2003, I gave a talk in which I said, somewhat playfully, that if I had to put a label on my own theology I would call it *radical liberalism* rather than *post*liberalism or radical *orthodoxy*.[20] From time to time since then I have thought that this is an interesting idea that might be worth pursuing. I do not intend to pursue it principally by criticizing other theologies and their critiques of liberalism but by learning from them. I have always been impressed by the advice of Richard Niebuhr, who liked to quote F. D. Maurice to the effect that persons are generally right in what they affirm and wrong in what they deny.[21] To be sure, the liberal tradition has frequently been caricatured and stereotyped by its critics.[22] But there are valid criticisms of it, and one of the qualities of liberal theology is its openness to criticism, self-examination, and change. I am not an "impenitent liberal," as Alex Vidler remarked when he retired in 1967,[23] for I think that penitence is something that the liberal traditions must practice as profoundly as any other human enterprise. But I do believe that there remains a great resource of truth and insight in these traditions that should not be lost, and I happen to believe that the term *liberal* is wonderfully appropriate.

From the radical postmoderns, a radical liberalism accepts the critiques of philosophical foundationalism, cultural Eurocentrism, the erasure of difference, and the notion of God as a metaphysical "supreme being." From neoorthodox and postliberal theology it accepts the critiques of culture-Protestantism, evolutionary optimism, individualism, subjectivism, and antitraditionalism. It acknowledges with Richard Niebuhr the possibility of liberalism's "disinherited mind," the loss of fundamental principles of Christian faith—although Niebuhr adds that in the liberal theology of the nineteenth century there was far more continuity with the past and far less rejection of the great tradition than earlier critics ascribed to it.[24] If Gary Dorrien is right in suggesting, at the beginning of his magisterial history of American liberal theology, that in essence its idea is that "Christian theology can be genuinely Christian without being based upon external authority,"[25] then this idea needs modification. Theology cannot dispense with external authority and historical tradition, for without it (as Niebuhr points out) the mind has no capital with which to work; but tradition and authority must be critically evaluated, inwardly appropriated, and imaginatively reenvisioned.

From radical orthodoxy, radical liberalism learns that there is something intrinsically radical about theological claims, a radicalism that blocks any easy relationship with culture or academy. It acknowledges that (post)modern secularism is often materialistic, aggressive, and nihilistic, and it recognizes that much of the appeal of popular evangelical religion is to the longing on the part of people for meaning, value, and community in a soulless culture. Radical orthodoxy responds to one of the principal challenges of our time, that of secularism and nihilism, but not to the other (which is more evident in the United States than in Britain), that of fundamentalism and antimodernism. Thus, in contrast to radical orthodoxy, I believe that what needs radicalization is not orthodoxy in the form of patristic creeds and medieval practices but the *liberality* at the heart of the gospel—a liberality that demands openness to and mediation with the modern/postmodern world of which we are critical, and that blocks imperialistic theological claims. Liberal theology is driven to its roots by the crises and traumas of our time—the threat of mass destruction and terror, the increase in nationalism and political arrogance, the intensification of economic and social injustice, the endurance of prejudice based on race and gender, the mindless consumption of the privileged, the degradation of the environment, the conflicts between cultures and religions. A bland, accommodating, or methodologically preoccupied theology is inadequate in the face of these threats; and the term *revisionary* (which I myself have used in the past) seems too weak a description for the kind of liberal theology that is needed today. A *radical* vision, not merely a revisioning: let that be our goal.

The idea of a radical liberalism is not mine alone. At an American Academy of Religion Consultation on Liberal Theologies in November 2005,[26] Daniel McKanan raised the question, "Can there be a radical liberalism?" He pursued the question principally in historical terms, showing that a radical liberal tradition runs from the Enlightenment struggle against the absolutism of both state and church through the abolitionist, feminist, and socialist movements of the nineteenth century to the liberation theologies of the twentieth century. This tradition was borne mostly by activist, not academic, theologians outside the mainstream, but (he argues) they were close to the heart of liberal theology, which is not compromise but liberty and liberation. In a recent book Mark Lewis Taylor has addressed this question in political and economic terms.[27] Over against what he calls "contractual liberalism"—the main liberal strategy that has contracted freedom out to elites deemed worthy of it—he envisions a "radical liberalism" that depends on the rediscovery of the prophetic roots of liberalism in the English and American revolutions and turns to marginalized and oppressed groups as the primary forces of transformation. Taylor seems to have in mind the possibility of a theological as well as a political radical liberalism, of which he offers only enticing hints.

For my part, I want to pursue the question in theological rather than historical or political terms. What is the radical vision of liberal theology? Where does it find its root, its *radix*? Well, the *radix* of liberal theology (as of any good theology) is simply God—God who *is* freedom and who *gives* freedom or *sets free*. God *is* freedom, the One who is free, *das Freie,* as Hegel and Barth discovered (strange bedfellows for a liberal theology?). God is the One who is radically free, the One who loves in freedom, because God comes from godself and is at home with godself in God's other. Freedom means presence to self mediated through presence or openness to another, and the triune God is the perfect instantiation of freedom. But God also *gives* freedom or *sets free.* God's freedom is a generative freedom. God sets the created world free from nonbeing, from its "bondage to decay," and God sets human beings free from their subjection to sin and oppressive powers so that they might obtain to the "glorious freedom" of God's children. If you want a proof text for liberal theology, you can find it in the eighth chapter of the Epistle to the Romans. Not only there, of course, but in the Gospels: the central theme of Jesus' proclamation is that of God's kingdom or *basileia*—a metaphor that is appropriately translated by liberation theologians as God's *freedom project,* meaning the process and place wherein God's freedom rules in place of the normal arrangements of domination, retribution, and exchange. Here is the liberatory mandate at the heart of liberal theology. The word *liberal* (Lat.: *liberalis*) simply means something that is "fitted for freedom" and "makes for freedom," and as such it is a wonderfully appropriate term to designate the nature and content of theology. We should not give it up or qualify it, except by the term *radical,* which orients us to its true, root meaning. The task of the last section of this chapter is to spell out this idea in more detail.

Resources for this radical vision are present in the tradition of liberal theology from the beginning of the nineteenth century to the present. In any tradition, only a few thinkers achieve true greatness, the sort of greatness that breaks with the past and envisions something new, something bold and beautiful. Most of the theologians associated with the liberal theology movement in Germany, Britain, and the United States at the end of the nineteenth and the beginning of the twentieth centuries would not fall into this category. There were certainly some very competent thinkers, mostly forgotten or slandered,[28] and some near greats—Albrecht Ritschl and Adolf Harnack in Germany, Auguste Sabatier in France, Charles Gore and later William Temple in Britain, Walter Rauschenbusch and William

Adams Brown in the United States. But the tradition of liberal theology is not limited to these thinkers in this time period. It is much broader and deeper, going back to the Enlightenment and continuing to the present day; and it includes some truly great thinkers. My own list starts with the philosophical heritage of Immanuel Kant and especially Georg Wilhelm Friedrich Hegel, and it includes Friedrich Schleiermacher, Samuel Taylor Coleridge, Ferdinand Christian Baur, Horace Bushnell, Josiah Royce, and Ernst Troeltsch. These are the theologians and philosophers of the nineteenth and early twentieth centuries who have most influenced me. Hegel (as I shall explain shortly) is for me the true inspiration behind the whole idea of a radically liberal theology. Troeltsch in particular stands out as a model; his only partly executed reconstruction of theology at the beginning of the twentieth century might help to guide us into the twenty-first.[29] My list continues with Karl Barth, who offers surprising resources for a radically liberal theology from the perspective of his own neoorthodox or dialectical theology, and with several dialectical thinkers who continued to be deeply influenced by the liberal tradition despite (or even because of) neoorthodox critiques: Paul Tillich, Rudolf Bultmann, Reinhold Niebuhr, H. Richard Niebuhr, Paul Ricoeur, Gerhard Ebeling.

Coming closer to our own time, the revisionist theology associated with David Tracy, Langdon Gilkey, Gordon Kaufman, Edward Farley, Sallie McFague, and others stands very much in the liberal tradition. Process theology (Daniel Day Williams, Schubert Ogden, John Cobb) is a liberal theology with its roots in Alfred North Whitehead and Charles Hartshorne. Black, feminist, and liberation theologies, despite their criticisms of the liberal tradition, share many of its concerns, recontextualized in a much more diverse cultural situation. James Cone, Rosemary Radford Ruether, Gustavo Gutiérrez, and other bold thinkers have altered the course of theological reflection. The same is true of ecological theologies and comparative theologies oriented to religious pluralism. These are the resources upon which I shall draw as I think about the possibility of a radically liberal theology for today.[30]

Marks of a Liberal Theology for Today

Liberal theology is commonly identified too narrowly. Gary Dorrien quotes a definition by Daniel Day Williams that emphasizes "the evolutionist orientation, the social gospel ethos, and the cultural optimism that distinguished liberal Protestant theology during its late-nineteenth- and early-twentieth-century heyday."[31] As I have indicated, the liberal tradition is broad and deep, going back to the early nineteenth century, continuing until the present day, and embracing transnational and transconfessional articulations that are quite rich and diverse.

Dorrien proposes to define liberal theology as principally a mediating movement—mediating between faith and reason, tradition and culture, orthodoxy and modernism, seeking to find a "third way" that avoids the unacceptable alternatives of an authoritarian dogmatism and an aggressive secularism.[32] Mediation is certainly one of its marks, arguably even its principal one, but it is not the only mark. Taking into account both the broad sweep of liberalism's history and the exigencies faced by theology today, I identify six such marks. These marks stand in some tension with each other, and the ways in which the tension is resolved vary considerably. I think of "liberal" as a big tent within which a family of theologies live, work, and argue, respecting divergences and learning from them.

1. A Free and Open Theology

Liberal theology is above all a *free* theology—"a free theology of Catholic and Protestant modernism," as Ernst Troeltsch expressed it, meaning not only that it is free from the constraints of dogmatic orthodoxy and that it employs various critical methods that put it in touch with a broader intellectual life, but also that it has freedom as its central theological motif.[33] This is why the term *liberal* is so appropriate. It derives from the Latin *liberalis,* an adjective designating something that is *liber,* "free." The Latin word for "children," *liberi,* is related to *liber,* which suggests that freedom involves belonging to a community or family in which *libertas* prevails. Martha Nussbaum remarks that "liberal" means something that is *fitted for freedom* and *makes for freedom.*[34] As such the term has not only political and pedagogical[35] but also theological implications.

Theologically speaking, we should say that what fits us for freedom is the fact that we are children *of God,* not of a privileged family of the propertied class, which was the meaning in the context of Roman society (where only *some* were free). Above all it is *God* who is free, the One who *is* freedom and who *makes* for freedom or *gives* freedom. God's liberality is boundless, extending to all that God has made and to all of God's peoples. The children of God who are *fitted* for freedom in virtue of being created by God must also be *made* free in a twofold sense. First, freedom is something that is accomplished not all at once but through a lifelong process of cultivation and formation: we are educated into freedom by the divine pedagogy.[36] Second, we destroy or distort the freedom that is our birthright by acts of sin and evil that produce a bondage inflicted upon ourselves and others: we are saved for freedom by the divine redemption. As I have suggested and will discuss more fully below, God's generative freedom and the freedom of God's children constitute the very *radix* of liberal theology.

The freedom of liberal theology is not simply or primarily a negative freedom—freedom from the constraints of tradition, confession, institution, external authority—although such freedom is a necessary condition of truth and conscience.[37] More than that, it is a positive freedom—*freedom for, liberality toward,* or *openness to.*[38] Openness to what? To whatever presents itself or reveals itself in the Bible, in Christian tradition, and in the whole of experience—in personal experience, in nature, in one's own culture and religion, in the often-wrenching cultural transitions of one's own time, and in the great cultural and religious traditions of humankind as a whole.[39] Confidence in the gracious liberality of God[40] means that we can and must be open to wherever the marks of this liberality are displayed in nature, culture, and history. There is no single, foundational sign but a hermeneutical interplay of signs whereby truth, freedom, and grace are apprehended again and again by human beings in different times and places. For Christians, the signs center upon Christ but are not contained within Christ. An open theology is above all a theology of the Spirit.

In a recent book Andrew Shanks[41] argues for a "radical honesty" in theology, by which he means an openness to truth as it presents itself through the convictions and experiences of others. Truth as honesty is a quality of "sheer conversational *receptivity*," "a sheer love of openness to other points of view." As such it contrasts with what Shanks calls "sacred ideology" and "intellectual conceit." Sacred ideology is a fundamental impatience with the pursuit of truth, a lazy or dogmatic holding fast to the opinions of a certain tradition, a claim to be already in possession of correct opinion. "It is not, therefore, designed to stir people into deeper thoughtfulness . . . , but, rather, to stimulate and redirect already existent instincts, through flattery and menace." Intellectual conceit is the claim that truth consists in correct propositions or doctrines, and that one has these doctrines in a dogmatic or philosophical form. Shanks believes that the answer to the corruption of theology into sacred ideology lies in what Hegel calls "speculative thinking," which is a very radical kind of thinking that deconstructs all dogmatic claims. Absolute truth cannot be the *result* of reflective thinking but rather a *celebration* of what presents itself in the never-ending quest for truth. What presents itself is Spirit as "an emergent will to honesty," that is, as a radical openness or thoughtfulness, a "primal shakenness." Radical liberalism is rooted in radical honesty, in the primal shaking of Spirit.

2. A Critically Constructive Theology

Liberal theology is a *critical* theology. Such criticism is a by-product of its openness and radical honesty. In light of God's gracious liberality and the shaking power of the Spirit, theologians must be critical of all established orthodoxies, partial truths, seductive idolatries, and parochial judgments. Above all it was the historical-critical study of the Bible and church tradition that first pointed in this direction.[42] Subsequently other critical methods (psychological, sociological, literary, cultural) have been employed. Theologians must also learn to be self-critical, reminding themselves that all constructions and systems, including their own, are but human products, called forth in response to what presents itself in tradition and experience, but mirroring it only dimly. They must learn that it is always necessary to "think more" and "think boldly," never to rest content with what has been accomplished, in theory or in practice. Critical consciousness is a prophetic, iconoclastic consciousness, constantly aware of the deep difference between finite forms and infinite, inexhaustible truth. This is the Kantian element in liberal theology.[43] It certainly does not mean that liberal theology is indifferent to the truth and merely neutral, tolerant, permissive, or relativistic.[44] By contrast with this standard caricature, liberalism has a deep passion for truth but also recognizes the complexity of the question of truth. It knows that truth is often mixed with falsehood, that deep insight is combined with blindness to prejudice.[45]

Part of the work of thinking more and thinking boldly is to take up the task of *reconstruction* after every deconstruction.[46] The goal of liberal theology is not to destroy or lose the heritage of the past but to preserve and appreciate it; and it understands that this can be accomplished not by fruitlessly holding on to old forms but by allowing them to pass over into new and different ones. This requires a new construction, seeking new symbols to replace overused and outworn ones,[47] attending to new circumstances and new insights never imagined in the past. While such a construction is a human effort, if it is a genuine and honest effort and if we have faith in God's gracious liberality, we have grounds for confidence that our construction is a response to something real that is presenting itself. Truth will come out through the testing of these constructions in a community of free and open discourse. In the final analysis we have no alternative. We cannot know truth directly, and we cannot dwell humanly in the world without undertaking such constructions, fragile and fallible though they be. We cannot live simply with the silence of a negative theology but must strive for a balance between negation and affirmation, *apophasis* and *kataphasis*. Thus, it is appropriate and necessary that liberal theology should engage the task of systematic theology, and indeed it has done so throughout its history.

3. An Experiential Theology

Liberal theology is an *experiential* theology. This is certainly one of the classic marks of theological liberalism. The liberal theologians believed that all religion is rooted in experience, both immediate and mediated, concrete and universal. Experience is the matrix in which religion occurs.[48] This could be understood in a foundational way, as some postliberal critics have charged,[49] but it need not be. The matrix of experience is more like a web than a stable building. It is multidimensional and interactive, fluid and elastic. Theologians must be open to the totality of experience: empirical, sensible, emotional, intuitive, intellectual, aesthetic, cultural, revelatory. The revelation of God's gracious liberality occurs through certain root experiences that reverberate in history, are mediated by texts and traditions, and interact with the personal experience of interpreters and their communities.[50] Experience in all its forms, including those of emotions and feelings, puts us in touch with what is real, objective, powerful, abiding.[51] Schleiermacher was convinced that the feeling of utter dependence is elicited by the ultimate Whence and Whither of existence and is not a projection of a private state.[52] William James and Josiah Royce came to a similar conclusion, as have recent pragmatic theologies.

The fear of postliberal critics that the "experiential-expressivist" mode undermines the identity of Christianity by associating it with something that is common to all religion is unfounded. Schleiermacher made it clear that there are both universal and determinate elements in all religious experience, and that what distinctively identifies Christian consciousness is the way that it understands the antithesis between sin and grace. The "peculiar essence" of Christianity is that "in it everything is related to the redemption accomplished by Jesus of Nazareth."[53] Nearly half of his work on *The Christian Faith* is devoted to the doctrines of Christ and the Church. Another contention of postliberalism is that language has primacy over experience. But surely the relationship between the two is dialectical: experience does not become thematized for consciousness until it is expressed in linguistic form, and language arises out of experience and continuously interprets experience even as it creates an intellectual world that transcends experience.[54] Schleiermacher certainly recognized this reciprocity. He said that "Christian doctrines are accounts of the Christian religious affections set forth in speech." Without language there can be no theology and no accounting of religious affections (feelings, experience). And he devoted considerable attention to how language functions in giving theology a "scientific" form.[55]

The liberal theologians also recognized that there is a science of experience—a term that initially came from Hegel as a way of characterizing his phenomenology of spirit (as a science of the experience of consciousness), but that was appropriated by the new, empirical human sciences at the end of the nineteenth century—psychology and sociology of religion and comparative history of religions.[56] It is these sciences of religion that helped to fuel the emergence of religious studies in secular universities. A postmodern liberal theology must incorporate within itself the science of religion (including literary and cultural as well as historical, psychological, and sociological studies) as an essential critical moment, just as religious studies should incorporate within itself a theological engagement with the truth- and reality-claims of the faith traditions under investigation. Experience *critically engaged* can serve to mediate between religious and theological studies.[57] The goal here, as Troeltsch clearly recognized,[58] is to establish relations of *consonance* and *coherence* between science and religion, experience and faith, as opposed to a foundationalist deduction of one from the other, or a separation of them into hermetically sealed realms.

4. A Visionary Theology

Liberal theology is a *visionary, spiritual, holistic* theology. Vision entails an awareness and appreciation of the mystery beneath the real.[59] It represents the mystical dimension of theology by contrast with its empirical, experiential dimension; it entails intellectual as compared with sensible intuition, the ability to see or intuit or imagine the whole in the parts, the universal in the concrete. It requires a heightening of imagination, an ability to discern and interpret figures, to create new concepts out of revisioned symbols. The central symbol/concept for such a theology is that of "spirit," the integrating relational power of life and mind that comes from God and is God. If Schleiermacher is the modern patron saint of experiential theology, then Hegel and Coleridge are the modern saints of visionary, spiritual theology. The two strands come together in Troeltsch, clashing and fusing.

Theology can be visionary in both apophatic and kataphatic forms—both the negative theology of Pseudo-Dionysius and Kierkegaard and the speculative theology of Hegel. Its visions can be philosophical, spiritual, aesthetic, utopian, political, or a combination of these. What is called for in our time, I believe, is a postmetaphysical speculative-practical theology, one that can articulate a holistic ontological vision, an interpretation of reality that connects finite and infinite, nature and spirit, psyche and culture, the aesthetic and the ethical, the personal and the political, and that does so in the form of an open, nontotalizing metanarrative.[60] What is required is not simply a methodological or cultural-linguistic holism, as some postliberals claim,[61] but an ontological holism, perhaps even (God forbid!) an "ontotheological" holism, or, better, a "cosmotheandric" holism.[62] We do not need a singular genius to produce such a vision, helpful as that would be, but a group of people networking together. Given the enormity of the task in the greatly expanded horizons of postmodernity, it is hard to imagine how any individual could accomplish it alone. Whatever might be achieved along these lines today will have more the character of a collage or quilt, a bricolage, than of a finished tapestry. This is surely true of whatever threads I am able to contribute in later chapters.

5. A Culturally Transformative Theology

Liberal theology is a *prophetic, culturally transformative* theology. This is the ethical mandate of classical liberalism, radicalized by the postmodern critiques of late-modern bourgeois capitalist culture. Culture-Protestantism is no longer a possibility for us, if it ever was, and its evolutionary optimism was already severely criticized by Troeltsch. Troeltsch himself sought a new cultural synthesis, a *Neugestaltung*, a transformative ethic of cultural values.[63] His awareness of the colossal power of human evil and of the tragic dimension of existence led in his final writings to an ethic of struggle, patience, compromise, hope without illusions, realism without cynicism and despair. That good might, from time to time, be brought out of evil, that culture might be transformed, ambiguously and fragmentarily, requires faith in God's providence.[64]

The same hopeful realism, this same striving for human freedom and flourishing often in the face of overwhelming odds, is characteristic, I believe, of the greatest liberal thinkers. Among the greatest was Reinhold Niebuhr, who, despite his criticism of the liberal tradition, stood very much in it and was the most prophetic theological critic of early- and mid-twentieth-century American politics and society.[65] Paul Tillich played a similar role in relation to European politics and society (and later to American). He insisted that a critical-prophetic dimension must be present in every religion to protect against its own demonic tendencies. He called it the "Protestant principle"—"the guardian against the attempts of the finite and conditioned to usurp the place of the unconditional in thinking and acting. It is the prophetic judgment against religious pride, ecclesiastical arrogance, and secular self-sufficiency and their destructive consequences." It is "the judge of every religious and cultural reality, including the religion and culture which calls itself 'Protestant.'"[66] In the past forty years, the prophetic role has been taken over principally by black, feminist, liberation, and ecological theologies. Today liberal theology must also be a liberation theology. The very name *liberal,* "making for freedom," requires it. In terms of Richard Niebuhr's Christ-and-culture typology, it is neither the "Christ of culture" nor "Christ and culture in paradox" that fits this deeper liberal tradition but "Christ the transformer of culture."[67]

I believe that the transformation works both ways. Despite its negative features, there are some transformative potentialities in postmodern culture. Good theology ought to be able to identify these elements, strengthen them, work with them, separate them from the cultural dross that clings to them. God's truth is being revealed through them as well as through theological sources, heterodox as well as orthodox. In an earlier book I sought to identify three of these elements—the emancipatory, the ecological, and the dialogical quests of our time—and to bring the resources they offer to bear in a revisioned constructive theology.[68] Each of them requires us to think about God, Christ, and the Spirit differently and with new insight. The transformer is transformed in the process of transforming: Is this not what a theology of incarnation that takes seriously God's embodiment in the world requires? The churches for the most part have not been receptive to these cultural quests and have often resisted them, fighting rearguard battles against forces of change.

The work of cultural transformation is the responsibility not only of religion but also of politics, the arts, and education. These seem to be failing as miserably in our time as religion itself. This is why we sense a deep cultural crisis. Politics has become a game of power, image, and deception with no social responsibility; the arts have been displaced by media and entertainment; education has been riven by culture wars and reduced to a marketable commodity. Religion has the potential of playing a prophetic role within each of these other cultural activities. Whether it will actually do so depends on our determination to make it happen.

6. A Mediating Theology

Finally, and perhaps most importantly, liberal theology is a *mediating* or *correlational* theology. Everything is related and thus necessarily correlated. This has been one of the marks of liberalism from the beginning and it characterizes the work of its most creative theologians, from Schleiermacher and Hegel through Troeltsch and Tillich[69] to the present time. Without mediation, without actual engagement in the messy realities of the world, cultural transformation is not a possibility. Edward Farley suggests that at the heart of the liberal project is the question of how faith enters into, modifies, and is affected by the ways in which the world works. Divine activity meshes with what is going on in the world. "Liberal theology will be constantly and necessarily engaged with accounts of how the world works, with sciences, philosophy, aesthetics, poetry, history, not so much to make peace with these accounts, but to use them to uncover the messy mesh of faith's world-embeddedness."[70]

Mediation on the part of liberal theology may be suspected from a postliberal or radically orthodox perspective of being a compromising capitulation to culture. However, genuine mediation does not mean compromise and capitulation but balance and insight. Daniel McKanan remarks that the purpose of mediation between church and culture is "not to find wishy-washy middle ground, but to allow each to pose prophetic challenges to the other." He suggests that by refusing mediation radical orthodoxy cuts off the possibility of prophetic wisdom arising from culture, and it is blind to the tyranny that is often still alive and well in the church.[71]

Mediation, I believe, is required by the *radix* of theology, the God who *is* free and *gives* freedom. God alone is the one and whole truth, the only genuine source of freedom. Thus, every finite truth and every finite practice of freedom is relative and incomplete.[72] In going to the root, we go between mutually negating alternatives, recognizing that validity is found on more than one side, that it is never simply a question of God *or* world, of Christ *or* culture, of faith *or* reason, of revelation *or* experience, of transcendence *or* immanence, of orthodoxy *or* heterodoxy, of self *or* community, of tragedy *or* redemption. The *radix* drives thought not to an extreme or unbalanced point but to a nourishing root, an original source, an integrating center, a final end. The popular usage of the word *radical* to designate something that is extreme or destructive or fanatic is really a deviation from its root meaning and reflects perhaps its political usage. Going to the root or basis of things may require fundamental (and in this sense "extreme") change, but only because things have become so unbalanced or uprooted. Of course, what is regarded as constituting the root or basis of things makes all the difference, as, for example, between radical orthodoxy and radical liberalism. In the view of the latter, truth comes out through the play of differences and their mediation. God is in the between, in the mediation between the differences. One version of this mediation is found in the Christian doctrine of incarnation, which is a fairly radical doctrine: God is not a static, transcendent beyond but is becoming God through interaction with and embodiment in the world. *How* this actually happens is the deep question that has occupied liberal theology for several generations and continues to do so.

The *Radix*: God's Generative Freedom

The *radix* of radically liberal theology (as of all good theology) is simply *God,* the One who *is* free and who *gives* freedom. The Apostle Paul touches on this theme in the eighth chapter of the Epistle to the Romans. He says that "all who are led by the Spirit of God are children of God. For you did not receive a spirit of slavery to fall back into fear, but you have received a spirit of adoption" (8:14-15). The Spirit of God is a spirit of freedom, not of slavery, and as such it adopts us as children of God, as "heirs of God and joint heirs with Christ" (8:17). Heirs of what? Well, despite the sufferings of the present time and the "futility" to which the creation has been subjected, these very conditions are signs of hope "that the creation itself will be set free from its bondage to decay and will obtain the freedom of the glory of the children of God" (8:21).[73] What we are to inherit, along with the whole of creation, is God's own glorious freedom. Why creation should have been subjected to futility, what its bondage to decay entails, and how God's freedom is actually inherited are matters to be considered in due course.

Hegel identifies "freedom" as an attribute of God. God is *das Freie,* "the free," the One who is free. As the One who is absolutely free, God is free to "release" the other, the world, to exist as a free and independent being.[74] Indeed, *only* the One who is absolutely free is able to release (or create) an other that is free and independent of itself without being diminished in the act of creation. God's freedom is superabundant, inexhaustibly generative, and thus it is not used up by being shared. Our freedom, being finite, is limited and threatened by the freedom of others; this is the fundamental dilemma of the human condition. Already it is evident that true freedom is not simply a matter of independence, of being unconditioned, of being present to oneself. It is also, and more profoundly, a matter of being present to an other, of being in relation with an other, of gaining oneself by giving oneself to an other.

Thus, freedom is a very dynamic concept. It certainly is for Hegel. To say that God is the One who is absolutely free means that God lives in relationship both to godself and to that which is other than God, the world. God's inner self-relatedness constitutes what the tradition called the immanent Trinity. God is already inwardly an other to godself—the eternal Son of the eternal Father—and this inner self-relatedness is the condition of possibility of God's being outwardly related to the world without losing godself (although there is a sense in which God *does* lose godself on the cross). The outer relatedness is what the tradition called the "economic" Trinity, which refers to God's saving presence in the world, but for Hegel is better named the "inclusive" or "holistic" Trinity, which means that God's self-relatedness is a moment or element in the encompassing process of God's relatedness to the world. Rather than two separate Trinities, immanent and economic, there is one inclusive Trinity, or a Trinity within a Trinity. In giving godself to the world as the historical, crucified Son, the abstractly self-related Father-God becomes concretely other-related and returns to godself as Spirit. In Hegel's words: "The abstractness of the Father is given up in the Son—this then is death. But the negation of this negation is the unity of Father and Son—love, or the Spirit."[75] "Spirit," with its fluid, dynamic relationality, is the most inclusive and adequate name for God, suspending "Father" and "Son." As absolute (or "absolving"[76]) Spirit, God is this trinitarian process of self-giving and self-gaining, of differentiation from self and return to self. And as such God is not only absolute freedom but absolute love (the negation of the negation of death). The conjoining of love and freedom is very important, for it means that freedom is not some abstract quality of divine transcendence or arbitrary choice but of being for an other. God's freedom is a *loving* freedom, and God's love is a *free* love. As such God is personal, the supremely free and loving person who subsists in a trinity of personifications or gestalts.[77]

Hegel is a radical thinker of freedom and as such he is a prime resource for a radically liberal theology. He calls Christianity the absolute or consummate religion of *freedom* because in it we know that we are related to something other or objective (God, fellow human beings) without the other being alien.[78] Freedom presupposes difference, and under the conditions of finitude difference becomes alienating. The alienation entails a rupture in the relationship of divinity and humanity, which calls for reconciliation, and thus Christianity is likewise (for Hegel) the religion of *reconciliation*. This reconciliation becomes actual, is accomplished, through the life and death of Christ in whom God is radically present. The alienation also entails a rupture in interhuman relations resulting in practices of slavery, oppression, injustice, and so forth. To address the latter, what is needed is emancipation from such practices, and Christianity takes on the aspect of a *liberatory* religion. Christianity is the religion in which *all* human beings are recognized to be free, not just *one* (the ancient Oriental monarchies) or *some* (Greek and Roman societies). The Christian church ought above all to be a communion of freedom, a community of free and equal subjects who live for and from the other.

Hegel did not articulate the liberatory aspect of Christianity as thoroughly as he did the reconciliatory aspect. He was, however, deeply concerned about social and political practices. He supported liberal political reform in Prussia in the 1820s, envisioned a constitutional monarchy with a representative assembly of "estates" as the most adequate form of government, opposed slavery and the restriction of civil liberties, and wrestled with the problem of poverty and other forms of social injustice caused by economic practices.[79] In his lectures on the philosophy of world history he set forth the grand theme that "world history is the progress of the consciousness of freedom."[80] This theme became the leitmotif of his last lectures on the philosophy of religion, those of 1831, where freedom is seen as the *telos* of the entire history of religions, culminating in Christianity as the religion of absolute freedom.[81]

Karl Barth is also a radical thinker of freedom. In a way that is surprisingly close to Hegel, he describes the being of God as that of "the One who loves in freedom."[82] This is his very suggestive formula for the Trinity. Love is associated with the figure of Christ and freedom with that of the Spirit—although through the *perichoresis* or interaction of the figures the attributes are also shared. By this formula Barth breaks with the tradition, which understood the two "processions" from God to be knowledge (Christ) and love (Spirit). He modifies the intellectualism of Western theology (with its focus on divine self-knowing) by introducing freedom into the divine life as an intrinsic quality of God. Just as God's love is a free love, not necessitated by anything outside of God, so God's freedom is a loving freedom, bound to and determined by compassion for the world. Barth writes: "God has the freedom to be present with that which is not God . . . in a way which utterly surpasses all that can be effected in regard to reciprocal presence, communion and fellowship between other beings." God's absoluteness signifies "not only [God's] freedom to transcend all that is other than [godself], but also [God's] freedom to be immanent within it." God is present to another "as the being of its being with the eternal faithfulness of which no creature is capable towards another."[83]

This insight is weakened by Barth's reluctance to acknowledge that that which is "not God" can and must be a moment within the divine life. If God is so immanent in the world as to be "the being of its being," then, as Hegel recognized, the world must be immanent in God as the nonbeing of God's being-in-becoming—for there is no divine becoming without nonbeing as well as being, finitude as well as infinitude. There must be a reciprocity between God and the world, even if (because God remains creator and the world created) it is asymmetrical. Barth draws back from this reciprocity and thus from the economic or worldly Trinity into the inner trinitarian relations between the Father and the Son. "The existence of the world is not needed in order that there should be otherness for [God]," because "God [godself] is the Son who is the basic truth of that which is other than God." "There are strictly speaking no Christian themes independent of Christology."[84] In the final analysis Barth's christocentrism seems to overwhelm and subvert an authentic trinitarianism. The Spirit remains an appendage to, a function of, the inwardly complete relations between the Father and the Son. Freedom remains more God's freedom than a gift of freedom that brings the world into play vis-à-vis God. The world is loved more than it is liberated. Perhaps liberation is too close to an anthropocentric motif. Anthropocentrism in Barth's view is the fatal weakness of post-Cartesian[85] theologies, especially liberal theology, and his entire theological mission was to guard against it.

Toward the end of his career, Barth reconsidered these questions. In 1960 he was asked to write an essay on what aspects of liberal theology he might deem viable today.[86] He says that he could fairly claim to be "a truly liberal theologian." He does not elaborate on this enticing remark. My hunch is that by "truly" he means "radically"; that is, a radically liberal theology is grounded in the freedom of God, not the freedom of humanity; or, more precisely, human beings are made free by God's freedom. Rather than actually taking up the agenda of such a liberal theology, however, Barth tells where he would look, or to whom he would turn, if he still were a liberal, as he once was in his youth. He would look first to the great Swiss liberal theologian Alois Emanuel Biedermann,[87] who was a disciple of Hegel. Despite his confidence in the human spirit, Biedermann never forgot the precedence and transcendence of the absolute Spirit, "of which the work of the finite spirit can only serve as a mirror, though it can and should serve as a bright mirror." Biedermann's program was a free theology, and he chose for its epigraph a phrase from Psalm 36:9, "In thy light we see light." "If I were a liberal theologian," writes Barth, "I should ask myself if it might not be salutary, even at the cost of having to go a good way along with Hegel, to take up [this program] afresh in its entirety." He would then look to Schleiermacher, and he is intrigued by the possibility that Schleiermacher's anthropocentric program might be interpreted as an attempt to construct a theology of the Holy Spirit, which would then shift theology from anthropocentrism to pneumatocentrism.[88] Such a shift would be a worthy challenge for a "neo-liberal" theology "not yet to be seen but (who knows?) destined to appear before, or even after, the year 2000!" Finally, he would turn to Martin Buber and Leonhard Ragaz for a theology "of our common humanity, of our existence seen as co-existence with our fellows. . . . To be anthropocentric need not mean to be egocentric." Egocentrism, he believes, has been the bane of Protestant theology, orthodox as well as liberal. At the end he quotes a remark by Franz Overbeck: "Theology can no longer be based on anything but daring."

So, might Barth's daring have led him to espouse a new or radical liberal theology that is pneumatocentric rather than anthropocentric (or christocentric), that understands human spirit to be a mirror of God's transcendent Spirit, and that is oriented to common humanity and freedom? In 1962 he gave lectures on "evangelical theology" in the United States. In the foreword to the American edition he wrote: "What we need on this and the other side of the Atlantic is not Thomism, Lutheranism, Calvinism, orthodoxy, religionism, existentialism, nor is it a return to Harnack and Troeltsch (and least of all is it 'Barthianism'!), but what I somewhat cryptically called in my little final speech at Chicago a 'theology of freedom' that looks ahead and strives forward."[89] Clearly, Barth saw this as a task for others, not himself. Had he been at the beginning rather than the end of his theological journey in the 1960s, who knows where it would have led him? In any event, we should follow his advice and look ahead to the challenge of articulating a theology of freedom as the appropriate agenda of any truly liberal theology.[90]

We learn from Hegel and Barth that human freedom is not an autonomous self-help project but is grounded in the gift of freedom by the God of freedom. This is a gift of the Spirit that empowers, not incapacitates, human spirits. God's freedom is a generative freedom. It generates processes of education and emancipation in human consciousness, history, and culture, and these are essential components of a theology of freedom. First, as I have said earlier, freedom is something that is accomplished not all at once but through a lifelong process of cultivation and formation: we are educated into freedom by the divine pedagogy. Theology is part of this pedagogy. Obviously this does not mean that theologians are passive instruments of the Holy Spirit. Rather, God teaches us through our own desire to know, driving us to think more and think boldly, to question established authorities and find new forms, and to heed the inner testimony of the Spirit. Second, as I have also mentioned, we destroy or distort the freedom that is our birthright by acts of sin and evil that produce a bondage inflicted upon ourselves and others: we must be saved for freedom by the divine redemption. The divine redemption does not happen automatically but through our becoming engaged in the central theme of Jesus' proclamation, the coming of God's kingdom or *basileia*—a metaphor that is appropriately translated by liberation theologians as God's *freedom project*,[91] meaning the process and place wherein God's freedom rules in place of the normal arrangements of domination, retribution, and exchange. Jesus is our companion and guide in this process. Redemption is something that he accomplishes not in place of us but with us and through us.

The pedagogical mandate of a radically liberal theology is to free central doctrines of Christian faith from dogmatic or antiquated forms and rethink their root meanings in relation to contemporary conceptualities and issues. The ways in which this can be done are as diverse as theologians themselves. Experimentation with different genres, styles, topics, and challenges is all to the good, for individual thinkers are able to take up only a small part of this large agenda. An approach that interests me is to look at some of the so-called contested sites of modernity/postmodernity and to ask how liberal theology might provide a mediation between competing alternatives that is not a compromise but a probing of the roots. So, for example: in the tension between heterodoxy and orthodoxy emerges a theology of God as living, fluid, shaping *Spirit*. Beyond the alternative of totality (identity) and infinity (difference) lies the possibility of a *wholeness* of Spirit that preserves difference, and of a *narrative* that holds together fractured stories in a history fraught with tragedy. Through tragedy comes a redemption that incorporates suffering and death into the life of God, a redemption accomplished by the crucified and risen *Christ*. Out of the tension between Christian identity and cultural relevance comes an understanding of Christ as the *transformer* of culture. In place of the autonomous self and alienated other a *community* struggles to form in which each individual exists for the sake and from the gift of others. Out of an inexhaustible religious diversity arises a community of religions that transcends any particular religion and entails an affirmation of religious *pluralism*. These mediating themes—Spirit, wholeness, narrative, Christ, transformation, community, pluralism—contribute to a liberal reconstruction of Christian faith for today. My development of them in the second chapter of this work appropriates what I have learned from my engagement with Hegel. This effort is not a repristination of Hegel but an attempt to think further and differently along lines suggested by him, and in relation to cultural circumstances that we face today.

The emancipatory mandate of a radically liberal theology is to bring freedom to bear on oppressed peoples, marginalized cultures/religions, and degraded nature, and to critique the political-economic structures that produce oppression, marginalization, and degradation. Here liberal theology embraces liberation theology in its several forms (African American, Latin American, Asian, feminist, womanist, gay/lesbian/bisexual, postcolonial) as well as ecological theology and comparative theology. The agendas that emerge from these theologies constitute a contemporary version of the "freedom project," which is an inexhaustibly wide and never-finished project. In the third chapter of this book I can only briefly and inadequately summarize a great wealth of material. My principal concern is to show how the emancipatory, ecological, and dialogical quests of our time can be understood to be part of liberal theology, and how the latter is radicalized, driven to its roots, by embracing them. In all of this, God's generative freedom is at work.

Chapter 2

Contested Sites and Liberal Mediation

THIS CHAPTER EXAMINES SEVERAL OF the contested sites of post-modernity and offers a mediation that draws upon resources from Hegel, the mediating thinker of modernity par excellence,[1] as well as other resources. The question underlying the chapter concerns the adequacy of these mediations for a radically liberal theology of today. Do the mediations attain to the *radix* that underlies the differences? Are they appropriate themes for a reconstruction of Christian theology oriented to God's generative freedom?

Serious engagement with Hegel is a departure for liberal theology, which, in terms of nineteenth-century origins, was shaped more by traditions going back to Kant and Schleiermacher, and was suspicious of philosophical influences of a speculative character. In the late nineteenth and early twentieth centuries, the philosophical orientation of American liberal thought was to neo-Kantianism, pragmatism, empiricism, or personalism. Whiteheadian and Hartshornian meta-physics was appropriated later by a diverse group of American process theologians; and existential, phenomenological, and hermeneutical philosophies have played a role with many thinkers. However, Hegel's influence has not been entirely absent. In addition to his nineteenth-century German and Swiss heirs (for instance, F. C. Baur, I. A. Dorner, A. E. Biedermann), he had an impact on later theologians as diverse as Ernst Troeltsch, Karl Barth, Paul Tillich, and Karl Rahner, although none was principally a Hegelian. The same was true of American liberal theologians such as Borden Parker Bowne, Douglas Clyde Macintosh, and Edgar S. Brightman. Hegelian ideas and problematics were in the air, but their source was often unacknowledged. Among American philosophers of religion, Josiah Royce and William E. Hocking were significant neo-Hegelian thinkers, and there was an important school of British idealism.[2]

No liberal theologian in recent years has, to my knowledge, undertaken an appropriation and modification of Hegel's thought. What I am proposing does not claim to be representative of mainstream liberalism. I assume, however, that liberalism is open to novelty and receptive of what may seem to be heterodox ideas. I turn to Hegel not on the basis of historical precedent but because of the intrinsic value of his thought for addressing the contested issues of our time—or so it seems to me after having studied his thought for many years. I place a proposal on the table for the sake of conversation and with the hope that Hegel might contribute to a more radical vision.

Heterodoxy and Orthodoxy: Spirit

1. What Are Orthodoxy and Heterodoxy?

One of the contested sites of postmodernity concerns the struggle between orthodoxy and heterodoxy. On the one side, postliberal and radically orthodox theologians advocate a return to normative criteria of orthodox theology. Postliberals claim that the established doctrines of the church define the rules or grammar of faith without which there can be no Christian identity. Radical orthodoxy claims that the creeds, councils, and theologies of the patristic and medieval periods have an authority that exceeds that of all later developments. On the other side, secular advocates of postmodernity call into question all religious traditions, while those interested in a postmodern form of religion question the "ontotheological" claims of orthodoxy, that is, claims that make God into a "supreme being" who exists rather like other beings. Some of these critics are attracted to heterodox or heretical elements of the Christian tradition, while others embrace agnosticism or atheism.

For liberal theology, atheism at least is not an option, but heterodoxy is, in the sense that all views that have contributed to the formation of the Christian tradition are of interest to it. The nineteenth-century historical theologian (and Hegelian) Ferdinand Christian Baur pointed out that orthodoxy simply represented the interpretation of doctrines that prevailed in the history of the church, while heterodoxy and heresy were the interpretations that were defeated, marginalized, or crushed. His thesis is that Christian doctrine and Christian institutions have developed through oppositions and controversies. Without opposition, there would be nothing that drives thought to new forms and insights. From a speculative point of view one can see that all sides of a conflict (at least of a serious conflict) contain truth, and that all sides contribute to a further shaping of Christian doctrine, although not necessarily equally. However, from the perspective of the victors in theological conflicts, who were motivated by ecclesiastical and political interests as well as truth, once a matter was resolved by a definitive ruling only one of the conflicting views could be regarded as true and the others must be rejected as false. Not only could the defeated opinions and parties not be allowed even to exist in the church (or the state), but also long-dead theologians such as Origen whose opinions were later viewed as offensive had to be condemned. The need for certainty in respect to salvation required an externally fixed faith and an absolute church. One of the fundamental assumptions was that dogma itself does not change, that truth is one, and that truth is always what comes first while errors creep in later. What may seem to be a new development in doctrine is, if it is deemed orthodox, already implicit from the beginning. Thus, ironically, it would seem that the history of dogma can only be a history of heresies since "history" is not something that happens to an unchanging tradition. This view prevailed up to and through the Reformation and was not seriously challenged until the eighteenth century.[3]

But, of course, from the point of view of historical-critical consciousness we know that Christian doctrine, like everything else in history, changes and develops, and that conflicts and their resolution have driven the history of the church up to the present time. When one side in a controversy is defeated or silenced, something valuable is lost; the truth that it contains is driven underground, although it may emerge again later. Thus, for example, the movement known as Arianism, which was condemned at the Council of Nicaea in 325, subordinated the Son to the Father and regarded him as a superior creature because of its conviction that the essential human reality of Christ must be maintained. This conviction was valid even if its understanding of the relationship between the finite and the infinite was inadequate and its postulation of a *tertium quid*, a "third being," between God and humanity was unconvincing. Its authentic insight was articulated more adequately by the Antiochene christology, and later by Augustinianism.[4]

2. The Doctrine of the Spirit[5]

All the doctrines of the church have been shaped by conflicts between opposing views, which in the course of resolution came to be defined as orthodox or heterodox. But with the doctrine of the Holy Spirit heterodoxy has played an especially important role. This is because orthodoxy in the Western tradition (Protestant as well as Catholic) emphasized, in George Hendry's words, that "the function of the Spirit is essentially subservient and instrumental to the work of the incarnate Christ."[6] Appeals to scripture were used to justify this view, but it was also driven by political and ecclesiastical interests because of the potentially subversive effect of spiritually oriented theologies. According to Hendry, who is a good modern representative of such a view, the primary danger is that the presence of the Spirit will come to be viewed as superseding the presence of Christ; this is "the spiritualist heresy which has plagued the Church repeatedly from the time of Montanus onward." To guard against this heresy, a modification of the Nicene Creed was adopted at the Third Synod of Toledo in 589, specifying that the Holy Spirit proceeds "from the Father *and from the Son (filioque)*"—a modification not accepted by the Eastern church. This *filioque* assured the subordination of the Spirit to the Son in the West, guarding, says Hendry, against "the danger of an undefined, unregulated, and in the final count, unevangelical spirituality."[7]

This solution was resisted by a strong undercurrent of Western spiritualities, starting with Gnostics and Montanists, continuing on through medieval and early modern mysticism (Joachim of Fiore, Meister Eckhart, Jacob Boehme), spiritual women (Mechthild of Magdeburg, Teresa of Avila, Julian of Norwich), Protestant sects (Anabaptists, Quakers), right down to the present day. These movements sought a delicate balance between preserving the freedom of the Spirit and the love of Christ. Some of them did incline toward an unregulated and dangerous spirituality in which criteria for discerning the spirits are lost. But they reminded the mainstream church of the centrality of the experience of the presence of the Spirit in the life of Christians. And they kept open the possibility of a pneumatocentric as opposed to a christocentric or anthropocentric construal of Christian theology. Such a construal would draw upon both orthodox and heterodox elements of the tradition, and it might provide a way of helping to heal the fragmentation, alienation, and parochialism experienced in the modern world. If it could do so without subordinating Christ but rather by drawing him into the work of the Spirit as a coworker, so much the better.[8]

3. Hegel's Concept of God as Spirit

Hegel's speculative theology[9] has been criticized as "heterodoxy" by the right and as "ontotheology" by the left.[10] These terms of derision can be turned to good effect because Hegel's heterodox conception of spirit (*Geist*) enables him to reconstruct ontotheological claims in such a way as to overcome the negative aspects of metaphysical and theological orthodoxy. Hegelian *Geist* retrieves the truth of orthodoxy by drawing upon the resources of heterodoxy.

Hegel's project is orthodox insofar as it reestablishes the conditions of possibility of knowing God against the modern doctrine that nothing can be known of God. His philosophy of religion is a response to the challenge of theological agnosticism, which in his view undercuts the central conviction of orthodoxy that God makes godself known, that the nature of God is manifest in the world, and that human cognition is capable of grasping the idea of God. Beyond agnosticism lie atheism and secularism, and Hegel foresees the consequences of living in a godless world.[11]

At the same time, Hegel has little interest in the details of doctrinal history, and his construal of the Christian idea reflects an eclectic appropriation of the tradition, orthodox and heterodox. Much has been made of the influence on him of a heterodox trajectory going back to Valentinian Gnosticism and including such figures as Joachim of Fiore, Meister Eckhart, and Jacob Boehme.[12] While the Gnostic worldview with its metaphysical dualism and antipathy toward the natural world is fundamentally antithetical to Hegel, it is true, as Cyril O'Regan points out, that the Hegelian metanarrative reflects the influence of a Gnostic-mystical, as opposed to a Jewish, form of apocalyptic in that the various phases of divine manifestation are constitutive of divine identity and personhood. Narrative not merely affects the *oikonomia* but reaches into the divine life, which "undergoes a process of perfecting as it traverses the drama of fall, exile, and return."[13] Here something quite new is introduced into the Christian mainstream from one of its side currents.

The concept of spirit enables Hegel to reconstruct traditional ontotheological claims about God. The being of God (the *ontos* of *theos*) is not the being of pure immediacy (the emptiest of all philosophical categories, with which logic begins), or the being of abstract substance (Aristotle, Spinoza), or the being of the "supreme being" (orthodox and rational theologians, Kant, Schleiermacher). Rather, God's being is that of "spirit" (*Geist*) in the sense of energy, movement, life, mind, manifestation, the process of differentiation and reconciliation. Spirit is an act or narrative of self-revealing and self-realizing that generates relations by which the divine subjectivity is established and all that exists is brought into being.[14]

One of Hegel's keenest critics, the twentieth-century philosopher Emmanuel Levinas, points out that Martin Heidegger regarded onto-theology as the fate of the Western metaphysical tradition as a whole: by identifying God as a supreme being and as the foundation of beings, it obscures the difference between *being* as an event, power, or letting-be, and *beings* as worldly entities. It mundanizes God and avoids the thinking of being. Levinas asks: "Did onto-theo-logy's mistake consist in taking being for God, or rather in taking God for being?"[15] Heidegger assumed the former and thus sought to free being from the metaphysical God. Levinas assumes the latter and thus disconnects God from being: God signifies the other of being, and to know God philosophy must turn from ontology to ethics. To think God on the basis of ethics is to think the uncontainable, nonthematizable other, an infinite transcendence beyond any negative theology.[16]

Hegel's strategy differs from that of Heidegger and Levinas. Rather than disconnecting being and God, he rethinks being as spirit—a fluid, mobile, spiraling relationality—and he rethinks God as absolute/absolving spirit, thus breaking the logic of divine sovereignty and replacing it with the logic of divine subjectivity. Hegel's God is not the wholly other but the whole of wholes, the universal that embraces all otherness and difference. As spirit God is both substance and subject, power and person, life and mind, essence and existence. The abiding unity that forms God's infinite subjectivity does not dissolve differentia into sameness but holds them in a play of productive relationships, as symbolized by the play of the trinitarian persons. It is an infinite *inter*subjectivity.[17]

What makes God's spirit absolute and infinite is that all of its relationships occur within a divinely engendered community of recognition. The other that it absolves or releases does not become something beyond the range of absolute spirit, so to speak, such that it would delimit the absolute and render it finite. God has real, reciprocal, mutually affective relations with the world, and the real other of the economic (or inclusive) Trinity is not the same as the logical other of the immanent Trinity. The other that God releases is something genuinely other than God, something finite and contingent, subject to the categories of space and time. But this otherness is at the same time not severed from the divine life: finitude becomes a moment in the life of spirit, and the result of the creative release is not a dualism that externally limits God or makes God one of two; nor is it a monism that collapses everything into the divine subject. Recognition preserves both identity and difference, and recognition constitutes a community of freedom. The extraordinary thing about God as absolute spirit is that God encompasses what is not-God within God, and preserves it as not-God. Can this Hegelian holism escape the Levinasian charge of "totalizing" or the orthodox charge of "pantheism"?

4. The Holism of Spirit

To answer this question, which is the task of the next section, further reflections on the nature of spirit may help.[18] Spirit is a cosmotheandric concept, one that links *cosmos* (or nature), *theos,* and *anthropos.*[19] Does it link them in such a way that it preserves their differences while serving as their bond?

The metaphor at the root of the word for "spirit" is wind, moving air, breath or breathing. Other natural elements have traditionally been associated with it, such as fire, light, and water. These are material images of an immaterial vitality. They represent spirit as a fluid, pervasive, intangible energy that enlivens and shapes everything that exists and that has freedom as its fundamental quality, blowing where and how it will, burning without consuming, illuminating without been seen, pouring inexhaustibly. In indigeneous religions the natural world is believed to be filled with this spiritual energy, which dwells in animals, plants, trees, rivers, oceans, mountains, volcanoes, stars, planets. In nature, spirit appears in isolation, and diverse parts of the universe call and reach out to one another in a cacophony of voices. They are the voices of spirit coalescing, of spirits witnessing to God's Spirit. But in nature God's Spirit has not yet found a fully spiritual counterpart.

Such a counterpart appears with the evolution of human beings as free and self-conscious persons. Here the life-giving energy of spirit takes on the aspect of wisdom, intelligibility, reason. In the Hebraic tradition "spirit," "wisdom," and "word" are closely linked, a linkage contained also in the German *Geist,* which means "mind" as well as "spirit." When spirit enlivens human nature, the result is consciousness, which is at once physiological and psychological. It arises from the incredible system of synapses that is the brain, yet produces language, freedom, communication, centered personhood, self-relatedness mediated through other-relatedness. The essence of consciousness and selfhood is relationality. As personal selves or conscious subjects, we are an infinitely complex network of relationships—to our own bodies, to the material world, to our past experiences through memory, to other personal spiritual beings, to the sociocultural world, to the universal power of being and meaning. Spirit is no one thing in this network but the network itself, pure relationality.

God in and for godself is pure relationality, and thus God is ultimate and absolute spirit. But it is in relation to what is other than God, the world, that the spirituality of God becomes evident. In scripture "spirit" refers to that modality of divine activity whereby God indwells, empowers, energizes the forces of nature, the people of Israel, the Christian community, and individual persons. The Spirit is the indwelling power of God, which brings the natural and human worlds to consummation by bringing estranged and fallen beings back into everlasting, liberating communion with the one God who is Holy Spirit.

Holy Spirit is not something that exists in advance as a supernatural person of the godhead. There are no such preexisting persons in God but rather potentials for relationships that become actual when God creates the world. God does have a primordial self-relatedness, an inner complexity of identity-difference-mediation, but this relatedness should not be thought of mythologically as subsistent persons. The Spirit is an *emergent* person, generated from the interaction between God and the world, in the process of which the world is liberated and the divine play of love is perfected in the hard, costly labor of worldly love. The Spirit comes into being through the pouring out of God in the world. The ancient biblical metaphor of "pour-

ing" accords nicely with the idea of God as becoming in relation to
the world. The appropriate trinitarian formula is God-World-Spirit,
or God as World-Spirit, or God-in-Christ-in-the-World-as-Spirit.
The Spirit proceeds from the emerging love between God and the
world, and the Spirit becomes the power of reconciling freedom in
this differentiated love. Spirit is generated in the process of pouring;
it does not preexist the pouring as prepackaged power. Wind cannot
be boxed up; it happens when it blows. The blowing and pouring of
God's Spirit began with creation and continues as long as there is a
relationship between creator and creation.

In what sense is God personal? The inner-trinitarian relationships take on the character of personal subjects only in relation to
the world. God becomes Father/Mother as the creator; Christ is an
individual historical person who is involved in a network of relationships; the Spirit is a social subject, a community of persons. But God
as a whole is personal, not merely an ideal but a real person, the one
true and perfect person and the power of personhood, the "personi-
fying person."[20] What God personifies is not only God's creatures
but God's own self, and the divine self-personification takes place
through the creation of the world, the evolutionary process, the
emergence of human beings, the appearance of Christ, and the send-
ing of the Spirit. God is already and not yet personal: "already" in the
sense that ideal relations of consciousness subsist within the oneness
of God, "not yet" in the sense that the wholeness of God includes a
concrete historical presence in Christ and an emergent sociality of
which the Spirit is the figure.

These reflections attempt to go to the root of the concept of spirit,
and they offer a fairly radical reconstruction of a theology of the Spirit
for today. Whether they succeed in attaining some balance between
heterodox and orthodox resources is a matter for you, the reader, to
decide. I encourage you to reflect on these questions and to work
out your own theology of the Spirit. My principal point is that it is
at the interface of heterodoxy and orthodoxy that a new theology of
the Spirit emerges. What is offered here is a thought-experiment, an
attempt to "think more" and "think boldly," and in this way to follow the mandate of radical liberalism. Whether the holism of spirit

envisioned here succeeds in honoring differences while affirming the bond that holds the world together is a matter to be discussed in the next section. Clearly, spirit is not simply everything that is; such a view would be a spiritual pantheism. Rather, spirit is the soul-force that *indwells* all that is, giving each thing a mode of existence appropriate to it, moving each thing toward its perfection. The holism of spirit is cosmotheandric, which means that it appears in a rich diversity of forms that cannot be reduced to a totality. Nature in its inexhaustible detail stands out from God as the material universe with multiple centers. Human beings stand out from God as finite embodiments of spirit who fall into tragic, self-destructive conflicts precisely in virtue of their rationality and freedom. God as absolute and holy Spirit is the infinite wholeness that holds together all the multiplicity and heals all the broken parts.

Totality and Infinity: Wholeness

In his influential book, *Totality and Infinity*, Emmanuel Levinas criticizes the tendency of philosophical and theological systems to "totalize," that is, to blur the separateness or distinctiveness of things by locating them in a relationship in which they are copresent, become signs of each other, form an intelligible structure. Just this is what Hegel means by "the whole" or "the universal," and Hegel's system is the prime example of totalizing from Levinas's perspective. For Levinas subjectivity depends not on mutual relations, as it does for Hegel, but on exteriority, disconnection, mutual transcendence. Truth is not a union of the knower and known but a form of contact without participation. One person is not defined by the recognition of another; rather, revelation, the expression of the face, replaces recognition in a relationship of asymmetry.[21]

The contrast between the two thinkers is perhaps greatest at the point of interpreting the "absoluteness" of the infinite God. For Levinas, any real relationship to the absolute would render it relative. Hence, he writes that absoluteness "'absolves' itself from the relation in which it presents itself, preserving its transcendence, its infinity." "The same and the other at the same time maintain themselves in relationship and *absolve* themselves from this relation, remain absolutely separated. The idea of infinity requires this separation."[22] For Hegel, divine absolution means just the reverse: the absolute releases itself into real relations with the other, becoming absolute not in separation but in communion.[23] The difference is between an individual and a social ontology. Levinas's individualism is evident from his statement that individuals "stand out in themselves, breaking through, rending their forms, are not resolved into the relations that link them up to the totality." This standing out and rending is symbolized by the nudity of the face. Over against the privileging of unity from Parmenides to Spinoza to Hegel, Levinas embraces the atomism of Leibniz and the exteriority of Descartes.[24]

What stake does liberal theology have in this debate? For much of Christian as well as Jewish theology, the relationship between infinite and finite, creator and creature, must indeed be conceived as one of radical exteriority: God is wholly other, not the whole that encompasses otherness. The question is whether there is an alternative to this view that does not simply reduce everything to sameness. Can there be a holism that avoids totalizing on the one side and the exteriority of infinitude on the other? Certainly, liberal theologians will come down on both sides of this question. Those who would endorse some form of holism include, among American thinkers, the transcendentalists, Bushnell, the personalists, the empiricists, and the process theologians. The heirs of Kant, Schleiermacher, and Ritschl would oppose it. Holism requires some sort of ontological or metaphysical articulation of the reality of God and of the relationship between God and the world. I believe that Hegel's social ontology and philosophy of spirit offer more adequate resources for this purpose than the alternatives favored by the mainstream of liberal theology. I have also been influenced by Paul Tillich, who fashioned his own form of theological holism, inspired more by Friedrich Schelling than by Hegel, although Hegel is everywhere present in his thought. My theological reading of Hegel is partly shaped by Tillich—not in the sense that Tillich offers an interpretation of Hegel but rather in the sense that intriguing similarities (as well as differences) exist between Tillich's system and Hegel's philosophical theology.

The Hegelian system can be interpreted as constituting a correspondence, not an identity, between the realm of the logical idea (theologically, God's ideal self-relatedness) and the realm of the real (nature and finite spirit). The system is closed in respect to its logical structure but open toward the empirical realm, which stands over against thought. Two senses of otherness may be distinguished: the logical (the other as self-othering) and the empirical (the other broken free in "utter dismemberment"[25]). The logical other and the empirical other are not the same. God's logical self-othering (the immanent Trinity) is a condition of empirical relations, for only an inwardly complex being such as the triune God can be affected by others without being limited or destroyed by them. For Hegel, in a reversal of the orthodox theological tradition, the economic or worldly Trinity subsumes or includes the immanent Trinity (hence, it is more properly spoken of as the inclusive Trinity); it is a production, the result of mediation between God and the world. History is not reduced to a sideshow but is constitutive of the divine life. Hegel's project is to give difference its due, and thus abstract identity is replaced by recognition. The Hegelian totality is the very antithesis of sameness, of totalitarian hegemony. In the holistic super-triad of logic-nature-spirit (or of God-world-humanity), no absolute primacy exists, no founding and grounding, no reduction of the other to the same, but rather, as Robert Williams puts it, "a non-foundationalist threefold mutual mediation" in which each of the three elements assumes the middle position and each is mediated by the others. [26]

This triple mediation means that the theological master narrative is relativized. God is, to be sure, the creator who releases the natural world into otherness and redeems fallen humanity. In this traditional version of the narrative (creation, fall, redemption, consummation) nature mediates between God and humanity, keeping them distinct. But Hegel claims it is also true that God mediates between nature and humanity, preventing their collapse into each other, and that God becomes a concrete, spiritual God through the mediation of nature and finite spirit. In other words, God is in mediating position as well as starting position, and is mediated as well as mediator. God is beginning, middle, and end; and God is God only in relation to what is not-God, nature and finite spirit. In this complex interaction God does not cease to be God (the absolute, the universal), but God *is* God only as a multifaceted wholeness that is cosmotheandric.

The wholeness that is God as absolute/absolving spirit is not the same as everything that exists, the empirical world as such. What exists, the world, is not-God, but it subsists within, or derives its power of being from, God. Such a view is properly called panentheism (all things *in* God), not pantheism (all things = God), which Hegel emphatically rejects. Rather, borrowing a category from Spinoza, he says that God is the substance or essence upon which everything depends for its existence. But he immediately adds that this substance is also internally concrete, it is substance as subject and spirit. God is not a mere soil out of which distinctions grow subsequently but an abiding unity in which distinctions are already potentially present. God is not an inert, abstract universal but an abundant, overflowing universal. He distinguishes between this abundant universality (*Allgemeinheit*) and the "collective totality" (*Allesheit*) with which the *pan* of pantheism is commonly confused. This is as close as Hegel comes to a specific critique of totalization. God is not everything (*Allesgötterei*) but "the All that remains utterly one," and as such is the negativity, not the apotheosis, of the finite. This negativity does not annihilate the finite but preserves it precisely as finite. Thus, Hegel insists on not only the subjectivity of God but also the empirical reality of the world.[27]

It is worth noting that spatial as well as temporal metaphors are inadequate for expressing the relationship between God and the world, but they are the best we have. Thus, to capture the dialectical character of the relationship, which is neither a monism nor a dualism, we have to say not only that all things are in God (derive their being from God, subsist within the divine milieu) but also that God is in all things (as the power or substance of their being). Likewise, we say not only that God's eternity transcends the modes of time but also that God is present in every moment of time and is a more radical and infinite temporality.

Just as absolute spirit is not a totalizing concept as Hegel conceives it, so also absolute knowledge is not.[28] Absolute knowledge is not an empirical state of affairs attained once and for all but an unending quest through countless determinate negations; it comprises all the endless and inexhaustible details of life. Absolving knowledge releases itself into the life-and-death struggle of history; it stands out from identity into difference. Similarly, absolute spirit is the determinacy that encompasses all determinations. The chief interest of philosophy, Hegel tells us, is the manner in which unity becomes determinate. The deepest and last of the determinations of unity is that of absolute spirit.[29]

The fundamental question is whether the Hegelian holism of spirit is still persuasive today. Hegel offers a vision of God as the encompassing, inexhaustible milieu of all that is—intellectual and material, eternal and temporal, infinite and finite. Nothing is outside of God, not even the most trivial and despicable. God encompasses what is not-God within God. All that comes about in the world, great good and terrible evil, is preserved in the divine life, even if only as negated and overcome. Spirit is the fluid that holds the matrix together and prevents it from becoming totalizing by continually generating and affirming difference. The prevailing view of postmodernity is that holism obscures the real differences, the power struggles, the conflicts and violence that drive the world as we know it.[30] The prevailing view of religious orthodoxy is that holism compromises the transcendence and omnipotence of God. For the sake of God or for the sake of the world, holism is rejected. But a holism of the spirit honors the inexhaustible generative power of God as well as the irreducible wealth of the world. Equally important, it keeps God and the world connected: God does not become an isolated supreme being forever contemplating godself; and the world does not drift endlessly into its own futility and decay. God actualizes godself in and through the world, and the world's destiny is one of consummation rather than destruction. The wholeness is fractured, yet it holds together. Because it is a living process, it requires the telling of a story.

Language and History: Narrative

The relations expressed by language, namely grammatical and logical, are synchronic in the sense that the meanings expressed by the relations do not depend on a chronological unfolding. The relations expressed by history as a sequence of events and actions are diachronic: they run through time. The tension between synchronicity and diachronicity is another of the contested sites of postmodernity. Which, if either, has priority, and how are they related? A mediation is provided by narrative, which is the telling of a story in such a way that sequential events take on the character of a plot; the story obtains intelligibility by breaking the dominance of *chronos* and introducing logical and linguistic connections that provide insight into reality. The empirical sequence of events is not simply arbitrary and contingent but has meaning. Meaning, for its part, takes on a narrative quality; it is not simply a synchronic pattern. History becomes narrative when it is told and interpreted. Narratives can of course be fictional as well as nonfictional. History and fiction both refer to the real, but in different ways—history on the basis of empirical research, fiction by means of imaginative construction and variation of the real. Theology itself is a kind of fiction.[31]

A true narrative expresses ideal, logical, or spiritual relations in terms of a story, a dynamic process, a movement through time. The story aspect is not simply extrinsic but tells something about the ideal relations themselves, which are not static but moving and alive. Cyril O'Regan suggests that Hegel offers a speculative redescription of the Christian metanarrative, which is essentially the narrative of the triune God unfolding.[32] The inclusive Trinity, as we have seen, encompasses God and the world together, overcoming classical dualism; and it introduces narrativity into the divine life, overcoming static conceptions of eternity. But Hegel's "speculative rewriting" occurs at a conceptual, not simply a representational level, and this means that narrative must be demythologized in the sense that sequential, spatially-temporally diffused metaphors and symbols must be thought through to a grasp of the primal logical structure that is expressing itself in them, that of universality-particularity-individuality or identity-difference-mediation—the syllogism that replicates itself throughout reality. Whether all stories exhibit a common formal depth structure is of course one of the contested issues of postmodernity. Clearly, for Hegel they do: narrative space is a discursive projection of logical space, but at the same time logical space is constituted by a refiguration of narrative space. Narrative is logicized, and logic is narratized.

O'Regan identifies certain "denarratizing operators" that enable Hegel to remove temporal sequence, contingency, and voluntarism from divine activity, and to break the narrative order of the master syllogism such that each of the elements (universal, particular, individual; or logical idea, nature, and spirit) assumes in turn the mediating role. The triple syllogism means that the metanarrative comprises a genuine interplay of God, nature, and humanity, but with priority given to God, the absolute idea, who remains the ultimate subject of becoming and the creator *ex nihilo*. Thus, the ontotheological narrative perdures conceptually, and it does so in a way that transcends popular religious imagination and overcomes rationalism/atheism. Hostile demythologizations are subverted. Narrative perdures in the sense that logico-conceptual space is a kind of contracted narrative (the dialectic of universal, particular, and individual tells a story), while narrative is an expanded syllogism (basic logical patterns replicate themselves in life). What underlies Hegel's view is a key assumption: that logic and life, language and history, synchronicity and diachronicity, are connected, that they share a common depth rationality. O'Regan suggests that the Indo-European linguistic embeddedness of narrative and knowledge is affirmed by Hegel over against purely formal and transcendental interpretations of knowledge. His revisionist view has more in common with the mystical and esoteric traditions than with rationalism and empiricism from Descartes to Kant.

Postmodernity assumes the loss of any legitimate metanarrative with its accompanying theodicy, and thus for it reality has no intelligibility. Hegel reconstructs the narrative by a friendly demythologization that overcomes the uncritical dogmatism of tradition.

From his point of view postmodernity would have to be seen as indulging its own hypercritical dogmatism. Hegel's reconstruction includes the terror of tragedy along with the triumph of redemption and meaning. Can tragedy and redemption be held together in a nondogmatic, narratively open fashion?

Tragedy and Redemption: Christ

Postmodernity, with its suspicion of any meaning-producing metanarrative and its orientation to the realities of power and violence, offers a worldview that is essentially tragic and ironic. Redemption is excluded as a final possibility. There may be individual acts of kindness and healing, but, as in the famous novel by Albert Camus, they will be overrun by relentless plague. Such a sensibility is deeply wounding to the human spirit. On the other side, Christian portrayals of redemption often display a triumphalism that avoids the tragedy at the heart of the human condition. Tragedy is excluded as a Christian category and is replaced by a theology of sin that focuses on personal guilt, divine punishment, and substitutionary atonement. A radically liberal theology must find a way to affirm both tragedy and redemption.

The Hegelian worldview is in part a tragic one. Robert Williams argues that Hegel prefers tragedy to the shallow optimism of the Enlightenment and the divine comedy of classical Christianity.[33] If there is a divine comedy, it is a tragicomedy, a story of the crucified God who undergoes the suffering and conflicts that render historical existence tragic. To affirm tragic suffering in God is a deep revision of classical metaphysics, which exempts God from the pathos of the world. In the *Phenomenology of Spirit* Hegel writes: "The [divine] play of love with itself . . . is . . . insipid if the seriousness, anguish, patience, and labor of the negative are lacking from it."[34] Negation and conflict are the condition of having a world of finite and free forces. Death haunts the cosmos, and Hegel identifies divine love not so much with reconciliation as with death. Yet through the infinite anguish of death comes the infinite love of reconciliation.

Human being is an internally unresolved contradiction caught between the pull of nature and the pull of spirit.[35] Nature is not evil as such but becomes a seat of evil when humans choose to remain in the natural state and refuse to realize their spiritual capacities. Evil requires the ability to decide: humans *become* good or evil as they rise out of nature. Instead of an original state of innocence, Hegel finds a tragic condition: the condition for the possibility of good includes the possibility of evil.[36] To rise out of nature and realize their spiritual potential, humans must undergo a cleavage or separation that produces anxiety, estrangement, efforts at self-securing. Knowledge both makes and wounds a human being; cognition posits the antithesis in which evil is found. Estrangement and reconciliation have the same source: consciousness, cognition, cleavage.

Not only personal history but also social and religious history are tragic. As Hegel remarks in the *Phenomenology,* the history of religion yields the pretentious claim of the Romans that "the self is absolute being."[37] The reduction of everything to subjectivity and self-satisfaction is seen in signs of modern decadence: profanization, privatization, loss of common life, loss of knowledge of God, finitude turned in upon itself. Our age is very much like that of the Romans.[38] In this respect Hegel is looking backward, not forward. He does not anticipate the terrifying forms of dehumanization that have appeared in late modernity. The problem is not simply one of privatization and self-centeredness but of a capacity for violence and destructiveness that is not fully addressed by the Hegelian anthropology. Evil assumes a dynamism that outstrips the capacity of reason; absurdity and chaos point to a dimension of the irrational and uncontrollable. Such a claim need not lead to a dualism in which evil becomes a supernatural, cosmic power, but it requires deepening Hegel's own understanding of the interplay of the rational and the irrational, of the role of emotion, desire, and illusion in human life, and of the demonic in history.

Are we still able to affirm with Hegel that "spirit has the power to undo evil"?[39] Spirit is a power greater than evil, greater even than death. For an age such as ours that venerates death as the greatest power, this seems to be a wildly optimistic claim. But perhaps our tendency to totalize death simply feeds a comfortable cynicism and fails to recognize the actual complexity of things. If we look more closely, we see that evil can in fact be undone, that its effects can be reversed although the deeds themselves remain as part of an inexpungeable legacy. By remembering the evil and honoring its victims, we gain a certain transcendence over it and find resources to begin anew, to rebuild, to experience a new birth. Spirit is the power of rebirth, the inexhaustible movement by which opposing forces are reconciled and new connections established. It is inexhaustible because it is the power of God. Such conviction is at the heart of religious faith, and faith itself is the work of God's Spirit in and with the human spirit.

Reconciliation and redemption are the central themes of religion. Reconciliation overcomes a prior estrangement; redemption liberates from an attachment to idols and other forms of bondage. They are the bringing forth in actuality of the unity of God and humanity that is eternally present in the divine life. For this to be accomplished, actual practices of freedom and liberation must occur in history, and God must be involved in the practices because the power of reconciliation is God's power, not worldly power. Reconciliation in the form of freedom becomes the great work of God in history.

God's involvement in history focuses on the figure of Christ for the Christian religion. Hegel's theology of spirit does not bypass christology but provides a different interpretative perspective on it.[40] The themes of reconciliation and incarnation are interchangeable because incarnation means the actualized unity of divine and human nature. This unity, which is the ground of reconciliation, must appear, must come forth from the godhead into the anguish of history. "Spirit is the absolute power to endure this anguish."[41] There is a divine necessity to appear and a human necessity for a concrete sensible presence of divinity. Hegel advances arguments for the appearance or incarnation of divine-human unity in (a) human individuality as such, (b) a single human being, (c) a particular human being, who is Jesus of Nazareth. However we assess the validity of these arguments, they attest to the power of the principle of positivity in Hegel's thought. The universal is an abstraction apart from its concrete instantiations, and its normative instantiation must be singular.

In this respect Hegel's christology is quite orthodox. But the construal of incarnation as appearance, as manifestation or revelation, is not so orthodox. Having a literal divine nature is not what makes Jesus to be the Christ but rather his function as revealer of divinity and mediator of reconciliation; he is the one filled by the power of the Spirit to manifest love and endure anguish. Thus, Hegel's focus is on the teaching and the death of Christ. The teaching is not simply of moral maxims. Rather, in virtue of its centering on radical love and its revolutionary reversal of established orders, it is prophetic teaching and as such is a proof of the truth of the divine idea that courses through his life. This is God's speaking, doing, working in a human being—not as an extrinsic miracle but as an inner empowerment.[42] This teacher is God as teacher, and as such he becomes the teacher and savior of humanity. Only faith can see that *God* is present in Christ, but the story of Christ, his sayings and deeds, confirm what faith sees.

The final deed of Christ is his death by crucifixion, which, from a human perspective, is the shameful death of a criminal, but from a religious or faith perspective is the death of God. God is involved in this; it is more than a human tragedy: it is a divine tragedy, a divine divestment, a release of divinity into the anguish and otherness of history. But because God as spirit has the power to endure this anguish, a reversal and transition occur. God suffers death yet overcomes death, brings it into the divine life as a negated moment. Resurrection is really a metaphor of the whole divine process of undergoing death and overcoming it, of bringing infinite love out of infinite anguish. On Hegel's interpretation it is not a physical miracle but a raising up, an exaltation, a return to God of not only individual believers but the community of faith. Resurrection is really a communal event more than it is an individual event. It extends the divine divestment, the losing of self for the sake of other, into the broad sweep of history. The shape of the cross becomes the pattern of intersubjectivity and social existence.

Christ and Culture: Transformation

How does this cruciform shape—the shape of Christ incarnate and crucified—interact with culture? This is not a question that Hegel explicitly addresses other than to say that the shape takes on communal form and then through the community of faith passes into the world. I shall address this communal shape in the next section, and with it the question of the relationship between self and community. But there is another, related question, which has become especially pressing for postmodern theology, namely that of the proper way of thinking of the relationship between Christ and culture, or (as it is sometime expressed) between Christian identity and cultural relevance. Which should have primacy, Christ or culture, identity or relevance? Or should they be balanced, and if so, how? Does Christ stand over against culture? Is Christ rather above culture? Or does Christ belong to culture? Are Christ and culture related paradoxically? Or is Christ the transformer of culture? An affirmative response to the latter option is the one to which Hegelianism points and also radical liberalism, but we shall have to ask how we get to this option, what it means, and how it is to be defended.

Here the influential book by H. Richard Niebuhr, *Christ and Culture,* is of great help.[43] Christ, however else he is to be interpreted, says Niebuhr, is a specific human being wholly oriented to God and to the mediation between God and humanity. Culture he defines in the broadest sense as the total process of human activity and the total results of such activity. Christ is the product of a particular religious culture, yet in his single-minded orientation to God leads human beings away from culture. From this tensive relationship between Christ and culture emerge five ways of construing the relationship, ways that have appeared in the history of Christianity and are current options as well. These are ideal types, which means that concrete positions may straddle more than one type.

Christ against culture is the type of mutual and total opposition.[44] Christ is seen as opposed to culture and requiring an either-or decision—the posture assumed by early Christians, medieval monastic orders, and modern radical sects. Such a view seems to be espoused by present-day evangelicals and conservatives, but their imperialistic claims about Christian culture and the American nation align them more with the type of Christ above culture. On the one hand, they are deeply critical of secular, humanistic culture and withdraw from it. On the other hand, their drive to christianize everything—Christian schools, Christian music, Christian food, Christian militias, Christian politics, Christian nation—points toward a view of Christ as the lord of society.

The *Christ of culture* type espouses a fundamental agreement between Christ and culture and views Jesus as the great hero of human cultural history.[45] He is both the product of human achievement and the contributor of the values that underlie Western civilization. Niebuhr associates this type with the "culture-Protestantism" of nineteenth-century liberal theology as represented above all by Albrecht Ritschl. Christ is "accommodated" to the criteria and values of modern culture, and Christianity is reduced to a "religion of humanity." While Niebuhr is critical of the stereotypical critiques of liberal theology, he himself has produced a stereotype,[46] perhaps by overly focusing on Ritschl as a representative, and he is not forthcoming about the extent to which he, too, ascribes to liberal values. His inclination is to be most critical of that to which he himself owes allegiance. It surely is misleading to suggest that liberal theology simply identifies Christ with culture, that it reduces Christianity to a religion of humanity, that it lacks critical perspective on and judgment of culture, and does not seek to transform it. The charge of "accommodation" has been adopted by conservatives, radically orthodox, and postliberals alike in their criticism of liberal theology. If accommodation means an uncritical surrender to secular values, or an unprincipled compromise of Christian claims to obtain favor with the cultured despisers of religion, then such accommodation is not worthy of liberal theology, and its greatest representatives (for instance, Schleiermacher and Troeltsch) are far removed from it. If accommodation means an attempt to make sense of Christian claims to a modern mentality, and an acceptance of valid ethical, political, and philosophical insights of modernity (critical rationality, freedom of conscience, human rights, religious tolerance, scientific method, democratic governance, and so forth), then such accommodation is a necessary feature of any theology that attempts a critical engagement with its cultural environment. Rather than "accommodation," however, it is better to speak of "mutual transformation."

Christ above culture views Christ as the fulfillment of cultural aspirations and the restorer of the institutions of true society.[47] While Christ is closely associated with culture (as in the second type), there is something about him that neither arises out of culture nor contributes directly to it. Culture may lead people to Christ, but only in so preliminary a fashion that a great leap is necessary, a leap from the natural into the supernatural realm. Christ enters into life from above with gifts that human aspiration has not envisioned and that human effort cannot attain apart from association with a supernatural society, the church, the heavenly kingdom. Niebuhr associates this type with medieval Catholic theology as represented by Thomas Aquinas. Present-day radical orthodoxy (Anglo-Catholic and Roman Catholic), with its vision of a Christian social order modeled on medieval institutions and patristic creeds, clearly exemplifies this type. The leap from the natural to the supernatural occurs through liturgy and eucharist. For conservative Protestant versions of this type, the leap occurs through conversion, the acceptance of Christ as one's personal lord and savior. For both versions, Christ rules over culture, and all cultures outside the domain of Christ (secular, humanist, Jewish, Muslim, Hindu, Buddhist, and so forth) are condemned or regarded as of lesser truth.

Christ and culture in paradox represents a form of dualism by contrast with the synthetic view of Christ above culture, the monism of the Christ of culture, and the separatism of Christ against culture.[48] The authority of both Christ and culture is recognized, but opposition between them is also accepted. Christians are subject to the tension of obedience to two authorities or kingdoms, which do not agree but must both be accepted. This paradoxical posture refuses to accommodate the claims of Christ to secular society and in that respect is like the Christ against culture type, but it differs from the latter in the conviction that obedience to God requires obedience to the institutions of society as well as obedience to a Christ who sits in judgment on that society. This type is classically associated with Martin Luther, and it is no accident that a contemporary Lutheran, George Lindbeck, is one of the founders of postliberalism, with its view that persons exist within discrete and incommensurate cultural-linguistic systems. In the construction of Christian identity any appropriation of culture outside the world constituted by biblical and doctrinal texts occurs only by means of a qualifier or "twist" provided by the Word of God, which transcends all cultures. This is the language of paradox rather than of mediation or correlation. A certain kind of transformation may occur, but it is a conversion of culture *to* Christ, not a transformation *of* culture as culture, and certainly not a mutual or reciprocal transformation of both Christ and culture.

Christ the transformer of culture is the type favored by Niebuhr, although he argues that validity is found in all the types and that no single Christian answer to the question of Christ and culture can be given.[49] Niebuhr's presentation of the fifth type initially seems to align it with the position of dualism or paradox, for he describes it in the language of "conversion," borrowed from the nineteenth-century Anglican theologian Frederick Denison Maurice—the conversion of culture from its sickness of spirit to the healing grace of God in Christ. This position accepts the radical distinction between God's work in Christ and humanity's work in culture, but it does not follow the road of exclusive Christianity into isolation from civilization or rejection of its institutions, as in the first type. Unlike the fourth type, it emphasizes the creative as well as the redemptive activity of God, and it recognizes that culture is a perverted good, not an inherent evil, and as such is capable of reorientation from self-centeredness to Christ-centeredness. With God all things are possible in history; indeed, God's transformative power is at work here and now, not in some remote future. "The conversionist, with his view of history as the present encounter with God in Christ, does not live so much in expectation of a final ending of the world of creation and culture as in an awareness of the power of the Lord to transform all things by lifting them up to himself." The movement of life that issues from Jesus Christ "is an upward movement, the rising of men's souls and deeds and thoughts in a mighty surge of adoration and glorification of the One who draws them to himself. This is what human culture can be—a transformed human life in and to the glory of God."[50]

Such statements indicate that for Niebuhr the fifth type does not entail a conversion of culture *to* specifically Christian piety, or the appropriation of cultural materials to the formation of Christian identity, as suggested by postliberal theologians. Rather, it entails a transformation *of* culture and of individuals by lifting them up to God through Christ. Redemption occurs not so much as atonement but as elevation; Christ is our helper, not our judge.[51] Culture is not christianized but fulfilled in its potential as a created good. This becomes especially clear in Niebuhr's discussion of Augustine's vision of the city of God—a vision that Augustine himself failed to artic-ulate consistently because of his doctrine of two cities and double predestination. Niebuhr writes:

> The possibility of the redirection of all [humanity's] works among temporal things into an activity glorifying God by rejoicing in and cultivating the beauty in [God's] creation, by rendering mutual service in the spirit of self-forgetful love, by scorning death and the fear of it in the conviction of divine power over death, by tracing out in disinterested reasoning the order and design of the creation and by using all temporal goods with sacramental reverence as incarnations and symbols of eternal words—this possibility rises to view in Augustinian thought only to be dismissed.[52]

What is offered here is a characteristically liberal vision of culture as transformed by being drawn into relationship with God the creator and redeemer. This is not a conversion from secular to sacred culture but an acknowledgment of the goods and values of the secular world (human activity, mutual service in love, courage, the beauty and design of creation) by affirming their role in glorifying God. They are centered not on themselves but on God. Or, as Niebuhr says in depicting the theology of Maurice, the universal divine possibility of redemption is the conversion of humankind from self-centeredness to Christ-centeredness.[53]

Had Niebuhr written "God-centeredness" rather than "Christ-centeredness," he would have produced a formula not only similar to one used by John Hick to describe the salvific process in religion,[54] but also more adequate to his own deep conviction. Niebuhr was suspicious of overly christocentric piety,[55] which is tempted to worship Christ rather than God. Christ is not God but a human being radically oriented to God and as such the *mediator* between God and humanity; this role, according to Niebuhr, is what is symbolized by the figure of the Son of God.[56] It is Christ who reorients us from self-centeredness to God-centeredness, and as such Christ is the transformer of culture. But, we must ask, is it only Christ who accomplishes this reordering? *Christ and Culture* certainly gives the impression that this was Niebuhr's conviction. However, had the book been written in an age more sensitive to religious pluralism and the redemptive power that is present in other religions, I suspect that Niebuhr would have moderated his Christ-centered piety even further. There exists a plurality of ways to God, of which Christ is one—for Christians, *the* way, but we can no longer claim the *only* way.

Niebuhr's christocentrism marks one respect in which a radically liberal theology for today must move beyond his thought. The other respect is his lack of recognition that transformation works both ways: not only does Christ transform culture, but also Christ and Christian identity are transformed by culture. If transformation is a truly mediating category, then its effects must be reciprocal. In fact, reciprocal or mutual transformation has been going on ever since there has been contact between Christ and culture. Early Christian formulations of the identity of Christ and his salvific role were shaped by the religio-cultural patterns of the time: Palestinian and Hellenistic Judaism, Gnosticism, Stoicism, Neoplatonism, other forms of Greek religion and philosophy. The same reciprocity has happened with every major paradigm shift in the history of Christian theology. Enlightenment ideas and values—critical rationality, personal freedom and rights, religious tolerance, democratic governance, equal justice—have been internalized by Christians and altered our perception of Christ. Any attempt to return to pre-Enlightenment conditions in these matters seems perverse. I believe that in our own time we must be open to the transformative potentials of other religious traditions, struggles for liberation on the part of oppressed and marginalized peoples, and heightened ecological consciousness. The Christian churches have not been attuned to these sources and have often resisted them, lagging behind the culture in recognizing basic rights and significant changes. Not only is this a tragic failing on the part of the church, but also it proves that the revelation of sacred truth, liberality, and justice is not limited to Christ and the Christian tradition. God speaks to us through many voices—Hindu, Buddhist, and Muslim as well as Jewish and Christian. Wisdom is present in indigenous religions, liberation movements, and postmodern cosmology. We must, of course, have discerning eyes and ears, for much of what is found in any culture is untrue, illiberal, and unjust. There is no infallible guide for exercising discernment, only the play of interpretations, the guidance of the Spirit, and the conversation that leads to consensus or disagreement. We cannot simply appeal to Christ as an authoritative standard for judging culture because our interpretations of Christ are always already shaped by cultural commitments.

Transformation is ultimately a social reality, as both Maurice and Niebuhr emphasized. The kingdom of God is a communal project having to do with altered relations among persons and between humanity and God. Without a new community we remain isolated selves and alienated others; and the very thing that Christ is about—the losing of self for the sake of other—does not happen.

Self and Other: Community

One of the traditional emphases of liberal theology has been on the autonomy of the self. Liberalism has tended to mistrust external authority, believing that nothing can be taken as true simply because an external authority such as the Bible, the church, or the state says that it is so. Following the philosophical tradition from Descartes to Kant, liberalism has characteristically turned to the subject and internalized authority, assuming that humans are free and morally responsible beings.[57] At the same time it has recognized that individuals are dependent on communities in various complex ways, even if the notion of the autonomous self retains a powerful hold on popular religious imagination. Deeper studies in the tradition of Marx, Dewey, Mead, Habermas, and others have shown that communities are not simply collections of autonomous individuals but have a primacy over and determine the quality of relations between selves.[58] Is this relationship one of hostility and conflict, or of merely instrumental arrangements, or of mutual recognition and shared suffering? Is the otherness of the other something to be honored and affirmed, or feared and rejected?

Presumably the Christian church constitutes a unique kind of community. Hegel certainly thinks so, and he offers a very rich description of what he calls the community of the Spirit, which embodies the infinite love that arises from infinite anguish.[59] This is the love that Christ portrays in his proclamation of God's kingdom or *basileia* and enacts in his own ministry and death. In the primitive community of faith a new kind of human bond or intersubjectivity forms in which distinctions based on power, position, sex, and wealth are renounced and self-possession is given up in favor of compassion, of suffering with and on behalf of others. Possessions are shared in a relationship more radical than friendship; marriage is the closest analogy in ordinary life. The bond of union derives from no human power but from the presence of the Spirit and its absolving love: it is in the Spirit that we are both one and many. Sacramental partaking or communion symbolizes this mystical union because what the sacrament enacts, the sacrificial death of Christ, gives the pattern of communal intersubjectivity—namely, divestment of self and recognition, forgiveness, and releasement of the other.[60]

For Hegel, selves are related not simply exteriorly but interiorly, each self entering into the constitution of the other self. Subjectivity is achieved by the losing of one's autonomous selfhood for the sake of the other, and finding one's communal selfhood in the other. Thus, genuine subjectivity is always already intersubjectivity. Hegel's interest is in the creation of a sociality in which otherness neither is reduced to sameness nor remains distanced in alienation.

The self-giving that forms the intersubjectivity of the community of faith is extended when the community itself gives up its inward spirituality for the sake of the redemption of the world. Hegel traces a movement from heart to church to ethical life, a movement that points to freedom as the *telos* of world history. The freedom of the *basileia* community passes into social, political, and intellectual freedom. Whether the religious community passes away in the process is one of the puzzles left by the ending of the *Lectures on the Philosophy of Religion*.[61] Hegel hardly places much confidence in the secular institutions of his time, and he is aware of a pervasive cultural decadence. While noting the incompatibility of slavery with Christianity, he does not in these lectures attend to other social injustices,[62] and he seems more preoccupied with the fate of the community of philosophy than with that of the community of faith or with the affairs of the world. For him, religion, like art, is mostly a thing of the past; and he does not glimpse the possibility of a religious renewal that might come through shared ethical struggles on the part of diverse religious traditions.

The freedom project, in our postmodern context, is not something that can be left to politics, economics, and education; it remains the responsibility of religious communities and quasi-religious movements, and they will be most effective when working together as a community of religions and movements. Whether this is a realistic possibility remains to be seen. We have to wonder whether any sort of community is possible under the conditions of postmodernity, given the fragmentation produced by identity politics, the market economy, the instrumentalizing of relations, and the commodification of resources. Community is grounded in the experience of the Spirit, which unifies without diminishing difference and diversity. Authentic community is a nonfragmented, nonalienated plurality.

Unity and Diversity: Pluralism

"The language of pluralism," writes Diana Eck, "is the language not just of difference but of engagement, involvement, and participation. It is the language of traffic, exchange, dialogue, and debate. It is the language of the symphony orchestra and the jazz ensemble."[63] Is this kind of pluralism encountered in Hegel's religious thought? The answer is both yes and no: the symphony version perhaps,[64] but not the jazz version. Discord is present, but it does not overwhelm the fundamental harmonies. Diversity is certainly engaged, debated, even celebrated, but only to a degree. In the final analysis, there is one God, one Christ, one Spirit, one consummate (Christian) religion, one concept of religion. The generative possibilities of a trinitarian theology of the Spirit are hinted at but not explored. A similar view is found in most Christian theologies, up to the present day.[65]

Yet, the geography of religions that Hegel actually offers in the second part of the *Lectures on the Philosophy of Religion* ("Determinate Religion") points in the direction of pluralism.[66] His philosophical history of religions grasps not the sequence of unfolding, as he intended, but the diversity of determinate forms in which the concept of religion appears, and thus it gives a kind of logical deduction of the necessity of religious pluralism. Just because spirit comes to itself through movement and distinction, there must be a diversity of historical religions, which emerge independently and do not form a unitary developmental pattern, even if they exhibit similar features. Yet it can be affirmed that what is common to the religions is that spirit is indeed coming to itself in them. While the consummation of spirit entails for Hegel a teleological process, this process need not be understood as a hierarchical one culminating in a single perfect exemplification. Hegel embraced the latter view, arguably against the intuition of his own logic; thus, he gave expression to European cultural hegemony and offered a concession to Christian orthodoxy. Is the Hegelian absolute to be construed as monolithic or as pluralistic? The texts can be read in different ways. On my reading, if God interacts with the world, God must take on the diversity of the world, just as the world takes on the oneness of God—a oneness that is not sameness but a perpetual play of many, unified in love. The Hegelian Spirit is one-in-many and many-in-one. Both oneness and manyness are to be affirmed. But where does the emphasis properly fall—for Hegel and for ourselves?

While Hegel's philosophy of religion fits the inclusivist model of interreligious dialogue, which holds that all religions find their fulfillment in the Christian religion, its depth logic is closer to pluralism. Hegel's dialectical way of thinking prevents closure on any cultural synthesis and keeps driving into the inexhaustible openness of the absolute. God disperses godself into the world as absolving spirit and is known in the mode of dispersal rather than finality. While a unification of religions in the Spirit may be an eschatological possibility, in history God's Spirit is always concrete. Hegel attends doggedly to this concreteness. A Hegelianism at the beginning of the twenty-first century readily acknowledges that the divine Spirit does not reach its goal in history, that Christianity belongs among other determinate religions on the path to consummation, and that the religion of freedom is a work in progress shaped by a diversity of cultural trajectories.

Freedom is the leitmotif of Hegel's philosophical history of religion, especially as set forth in his last lectures of 1831. Freedom comes to consciousness in diverse ways in all the higher religions, preeminently (for Hegel) in the Christian religion. We can accept this insight while avoiding Hegel's graded hierarchy and acknowledging that all religions, Christianity included, fall short of the realization of freedom.[67] The religion of freedom—an affirmation of God's radical freedom, nature's incipient freedom, and humanity's liberated freedom—is the theme of comparative theology as proposed in the final chapter.

The Pattern of Mediations

The mediations discussed in this chapter follow from various contested sites or tensive issues that rupture modern and postmodern consciousness. These are sites at which the validity of both sides of a polarity is recognized and a quest arises for mediation between them. The principal purpose of the chapter has been to show that the Hegelian form of mediation contributes to reflection on these issues by a liberal theology that seeks the roots wherein balance and nourishment lie.

The sites and the mediations are not simply arbitrary or random. They have a certain structure or pattern, and together they contribute to a reconstruction of Christian theology for today. I have tried to show how they are connected, how each theme follows from the preceding one and leads into the next. Beyond this, it seems that the first three mediations focus on God as Spirit and the second three on God in Christ.

Spirit is the root metaphor/concept by which the reality of God is to be grasped. It arises out of Christian tradition, heterodox as well as orthodox, and it has analogies in other religious traditions, notably Judaism, but also indigenous religions and the religions of Asia. Spirit is the immaterial, fluid force that generates the wholeness of the divine life and the interplay of God and the world. It is a wholeness that honors differences and prevents individual things from collapsing into sameness while also connecting them at a deep level. Because the whole is a living process, it requires the telling of a story. Spirit has a temporal as well as a spatial aspect. It produces a narrative, that of the trinitarian God unfolding. This is a metanarrative, the narrative that underlies all concrete and determinate stories. The narrative has a certain logical structure, but the structure takes on a tragic aspect when logical difference becomes real, alienated difference.

For Christians the story comes to focus on a concrete historical figure, Jesus Christ, in whom the tragic condition of the world is reenacted and redemption is accomplished, not through a substitutionary atonement but through the release of divine reconciling and liberating power into history. Jesus is the crucified teacher/savior of humanity. He transforms culture by reorienting it from self-centeredness to God-centeredness, by releasing its potential for good and restraining its potential for evil. At the same time he is transformed *by* culture since every appropriation of him is shaped by cultural interests and insights, including those deriving from cultures outside the orbit of Christianity. The transformation *of* culture occurs principally as the creation of a new kind of community in which each self finds itself by losing itself for the sake of others and thus is knit into a communal mutuality. This is a community of freedom, a manifestation of the *basileia* proclaimed by Jesus. The mediations of transformation and community point to the ethical challenge to liberal theology to become a liberation theology.

The last mediation follows from an aspect of contemporary culture—religious pluralism—that represents a new situation for Christian faith. I have argued, however, that pluralism is implicit in the concept of God as Spirit, for spirit comes to itself through movement and distinction. Spirit generates a diversity of determinate forms, which cannot be incorporated under the umbrella of any particular religion, but which can be understood as diverse concrescences of the freedom of spirit. The religion of freedom is not inimical to Christ if Christ is understood to be the radically free person who opens persons to truth and freedom wherever and however they are found. Liberal theology addresses this theme as comparative theology.

The mediations proposed in this chapter are not exhaustive. Others can and should be added in the always unfinished project of Christian theology. One omission in particular is noteworthy. In the tension between the material and the spiritual, the natural and the human, a mediation is required that would articulate a cosmology, a theory of *world* that unifies these aspects without reducing them to the same. Hegel's philosophy of nature points in this direction: spirit is present in nature where it slumbers in the modality of pre-selfhood and awakens when it comes to consciousness in animals and human beings. Natural forces, even those of physics and chemistry, are understood in organic, teleological terms. Hegel goes so far as to speak of the "liberation of nature," meaning not only its liberation from externality and contingency by discovering the presence of reason and spirit in it but also its liberation from being reduced to an object of human utility and consumption.[68] But Hegel's philosophy of nature is based on an antiquated natural science and cannot be renovated as the basis of a contemporary cosmology. Whitehead's cosmology is more adequate, but it predates quantum physics, microbiology, biochemistry, cognitive science, and so forth. What is needed is a new cosmology that is conversant with recent developments in natural science and that would understand how humanity is a product of nature yet transcends nature, how world encompasses materiality and ideality, exteriority and interiority, how the divine *energeia* works creatively through the entire cosmos. It would refuse false antitheses and reductive monisms. The philosophical basis for such a cosmology is lacking, and I am in no position to produce it.[69] The best I can do is to draw upon literature concerned with the relationship between religion and science and ecological theory, and I shall do so in the ensuing discussion of liberal theology as ecological theology. The theme of ecology emerges not only from cosmology but also from a theology of spirit and wholeness as articulated in earlier sections.

The mediations proposed in this chapter are not fixed and permanent. They, too, will become antitheses in new polarities requiring new efforts at mediation. The *radix* that is God transcends history but is present in history in shifting shapes that can never claim to be the whole and final truth. Each generation must rethink what has been handed down to it, learning in the process that the dialectic of thought never ceases. Even if a certain progression in insight occurs, one's own thoughts are not the best or last thoughts.

At several points, as we have seen, a theology of mediation that goes to the root of contested sites finds itself drawn into ethics, that is, into a discussion of the freedom project. This is the topic of the concluding chapter.

Chapter 3

The
Freedom
Project

FOR LIBERAL THEOLOGY THE ROOT of freedom is God's freedom—a
radical freedom that generates processes of education and emancipation in human culture. The theological mediations considered in the
preceding chapter are an example of the former, while the freedom
project taken up in the present chapter shares in the latter. Emancipation from the various forms of evil inflicted by human beings
on themselves and nature happens when persons become engaged
in the coming of God's kingdom or *basileia*—a metaphor that is
appropriately translated in today's context as God's "freedom project," meaning the process and place wherein God's freedom—the
freedom of love, forgiveness, and grace—prevails in place of the normal arrangements of domination, retribution, and exchange. Jesus,
who employs this metaphor centrally in his preaching, accomplishes
emancipation or redemption not in place of us but with us and

through us; he does not bring the kingdom on his own but gets us involved in the project. Of course, it is God who is involved in our involvement and God's power that empowers our always fragile and unfinished efforts.

Why does the freedom project focus on the particular arenas proposed in this chapter? The connection of liberal theology with liberation theology is or should be obvious, although a liberal theology that loses sight of its roots may very well be an impediment to liberation. The fact is that mainstream liberalism was shocked out of its complacency toward the realities of racism and sexism by the first manifestos of black and feminist theologians. Nor were mainstream thinkers especially quick to grasp the connection of liberal theology to ecological and comparative theologies. But these also relate to the freedom project. Ecological theology is engaged with the emancipation of nature from human destructiveness, and a comparative or dialogical theology of religions is concerned with how God's liberating Spirit is at work in the religions of the world. The theme of freedom is present in the emancipatory, ecological, and dialogical quests of our time. When liberal theology embraces these quests, it finds itself radicalized, driven to its roots. It also finds itself driven beyond the posture of classical theological liberalism, which, while committed to a social gospel, was largely insensitive to issues of race and gender, prioritized spirit over nature, and (with a few exceptions) assumed the superiority of Christianity over other religions and the triumph of Western (specifically Anglo-Saxon) civilization.

The quests represent arenas in which mutual transformation occurs between theology and culture. God's transformative power is at work in them apart from and in addition to Christian churches and theology. The quests are the products of diverse cultural factors in modernity and postmodernity, and often the culture has been ahead of the churches in recognizing new arenas for raising consciousness of freedom. Here culture is speaking a transformative word to Christians, but the latter also bring unique insights and resources to bear on the quests. A reciprocity between Christ and culture occurs when liberative, ecological, and dialogical movements are understood to be places where God and God's freedom are at work in the world today.

Liberal theology seeks to mediate this reciprocity in such a way that neither side is privileged and each learns from the other.[1]

Liberal Theology as Liberation Theology

The freedom project entails above all the emancipation of human beings and human culture from oppressions stemming from colonialism, racism, classism, gender discrimination, homophobia, xenophobia, nationalism, consumerism, violence, economic and political injustice, ecological exploitation; the list goes on. All the -isms and ideologies that drive society into terrible evils seem to be rooted in a more primordial human problem that the theological tradition calls "sin"—the sin of pride and idolatry, the sin of flight and fear, the sin of alienation from fellow beings. And sin in turn seems to be rooted in the threats and instabilities we experience as free and knowing but finite creatures struggling to survive in a hostile or indifferent environment.[2] The purpose of the present discussion is not to pursue these root factors but to examine ways that the concept of liberation has emerged and is integral to liberal theology.

The historical antecedents go back to the abolitionist, suffragist, and socialist movements of the nineteenth and early twentieth centuries. The leaders of these movements were the radical liberals of their time.[3] In the 1960s the civil rights and black power movements and the reforms following the Second Vatican Council sparked what came to be called liberation theology: African American, Latin American, and feminist. An awakening of consciousness—the awareness that conditions do not have to be as they now are—reverberated around the world and took shape in struggles against colonialism in Central and Eastern Europe, Africa, and Asia. The picture is more complex today as the awareness of new and diverse forms of oppression and of needed liberations has become more refined. But it is still worthwhile to look at the classic liberation theologies.

1. Latin American and Asian Liberation Theologies

The predominant reality of the two-thirds world is that of suffering and poverty, which are products of colonialism and classism on a global scale—the social, political, and economic stratification of cultures along the pattern of a core (the technological, post-industrial, capital-intensive nations of the so-called first world) and a periphery (the materials-producing, labor-intensive nations of the rest of the world). Thus, the experience of God in the theologies of Central and Latin America, Asia, Africa, and of marginalized groups in wealthy nations, arises directly from the experience of poverty and injustice. The fundamental affirmation is that God is found with the poor, on the underside of history, in solidarity with the oppressed.

Such an affirmation is found in the work of one of the first and still one of the greatest of the liberation theologians, the Peruvian priest Gustavo Gutiérrez.[4] The central questions he addresses are how God is encountered in history and how God acts in history. God is encountered in the neighbor, in doing justice to the poor and oppressed, in acts of charity. God is not a neutral observer but exercises a "preferential option for the poor," which does not diminish but concretizes the universality of God's love. God acts to liberate the poor and oppressed in and through their struggles for freedom and justice. Salvation is not something deferred to the end of history; it is happening here and now but in always fragmented and unfinished form. God's kingdom or freedom project fuels the emancipatory struggle but is not identical with it. Gutiérrez avoids both a dualism that juxtaposes two histories, profane and sacred, and a monism that identifies God with human liberation; in this respect he stands very much in the tradition of liberal theology. In another respect, however, he differs from liberalism by stressing that from his perspective the central problem is not that of finding ways of speaking about God in relation to nonbelief, which is the intellectual problem of modernity; rather, it is that of speaking of God in relation to "nonpersons"—"that is, those whom the prevailing social order does not acknowledge as persons: the poor, the exploited, those systematically and lawfully stripped of their human status, those who hardly know what a human being is." He believes that a distinctive spirituality and joy are found in the midst of poverty, a vitality in face of ever-present death, the expression of strong faith in songs, prayer, and thanksgiving, which enables people to endure terrible hardships and even to overcome them. The only theological explanation is that God is present with the poor. Those who are having intellectual problems about God might look to where the reality of God is actually being experienced, on the underside of history.[5] I do not think that Gutiérrez intends to trivialize the problem of nonbelief but rather to enlarge the horizon within which it can be usefully discussed. For him, too, the central question remains the reality and efficacy of God's presence in history—a question with which liberalism has struggled for over two centuries.[6] The question cannot be answered by a simple identification of God with a particular politics or program.

The Sri Lankan Jesuit Aloysius Pieris occupies in Asian theology a position comparable to Gutiérrez in Latin American theology.[7] Asia, he points out, shares with Latin America its poverty while what is special about it is its multifaceted religiousness, which makes it a dynamic meeting ground of religions today. Here dialogue among the religions takes place in relation to the political and social factors that produce poverty. A contrast must be drawn between the forced poverty imposed by the first world and the voluntary poverty that is at the heart of the monastic ideal and is part of the spiritual practice of Buddhism in particular. The objective of voluntary poverty must be to overcome forced poverty, not to tolerate or legitimate it. Here the encounter of Buddhism and Christianity can be especially productive if they join forces on "the one path of liberation." "Christians join Buddhists in their *gnostic detachment* (or the practice of voluntary poverty) and Buddhists join Christians in their *agapeic involvement* in the struggle against forced poverty."[8] Both *gnosis* and *agape*, wisdom and love, are necessary. Together they point to a "soteriological nucleus" or "liberative core" of religions, which can be thematized either theistically or nontheistically. The theistic form takes that of a trinity: the salvific "beyond" (*Theos*), a revelatory mediation in history (*Logos*), and the inner human receptiveness to saving power (*Pneuma*). Speech about God leads to Christian love;

silence about God leads to Buddhist wisdom. Both are necessary attitudes in the presence of the mystery of salvation and the reality of human suffering. In working out this mediation of love and wisdom, speech and silence, activism and contemplation, Pieris demonstrates an affinity to liberal theology even as he draws upon resources that are unfamiliar to it.

The first Latin American and Asian liberation theologies appeared over a quarter of a century ago. Conditions have not improved since then. The opening in the Roman Catholic Church occasioned by the Second Vatican Council and supported by many bishops came to a close during the papacy of John Paul II, and now even more decisively with that of Benedict XVI, who, when he was Cardinal Ratzinger, silenced several of the most prominent liberationist voices. With global free trade a new colonialism has emerged—not that of nations but of multinational corporations, which have moved hundreds of thousands of industrial and manufacturing jobs to sources of cheap labor in Central and South America and Asia. Wages and working conditions have improved only marginally in these countries, while at home countless good jobs (with benefits) have been lost and the industrial basis of the middle class is being destroyed. Even where there are still labor unions, new workers are earning considerably less than older ones. Profits may soar, but misery and poverty are spreading more broadly. Global living standards are not significantly rising, and wealth is becoming increasingly concentrated. Under these conditions one has to wonder about the efficacy of God's liberating activity on the part of the poor. A similar question has confronted African American theology.

2. African American Liberation Theologies

James Cone has been the predominant African American religious thinker since the end of the civil rights movement and the death of Martin Luther King Jr. His first book, *Black Theology and Black Power,* had a disruptive impact on theological liberalism comparable to that of Reinhold Niebuhr's *Moral Man and Immoral Society.*[9] Certainly there have been other notable voices, including especially those of womanist theologians (who combine the resources of black

and feminist theologies with their own experiences as black women),
but Cone has been a seminal figure. Two central themes emerge in
his work: the social location of theology and the image of God as
liberator of the oppressed. The first represents a critique of mainstream liberal theology. In *Black Theology and Black Power* he says
very brusquely that the white liberal is one who sees both sides of the
issue, shies away from extremism, verbalizes the right things, but is
still white to the core of his being and fails to realize that he has no
place in the struggle for black power—although there may be a place
for "radicals" who are prepared to risk life for freedom.[10] Cone's second theme connects his work with other liberation thinkers, with the
added factor of racism as the predominant cause of poverty, oppression, and injustice. His God exercises a preferential option not just
for the poor but for enslaved and downtrodden blacks in North
America and elsewhere. Just as God liberated the people of Israel
from their bondage in Egypt and to other nations, so also in modern
times God has liberated those who are in bondage because of their
racial and ethnic identities. They are God's chosen people.

But is this in fact the case? Doubts about this claim were raised
within the circle of black theology itself by William Jones, who
argues that it is impossible to reconcile belief in a God who is both
omnipotent and benevolent with the ongoing realities of black suffering and oppression.[11] Why would God allow a whole racial group
to be singled out as an object of disdain and hatred? Jones believes
that, in light of the enormity of evil prosecuted against them, blacks
are led to deny any sort of transcendent God and to embrace a
"humanocentric theism" that places the emancipatory struggle solely
on human shoulders. This is a telling criticism, one that must be
considered by every liberation theology: the historical facts do not
seem to be consistent with the theological claims.

In my view, the only way to refute Jones would be to argue that
African Americans have experienced and continue to experience the
liberating power of God *in and through* their unfinished emancipatory struggle. This argument is at the heart of Cone's theology. But
Jones contends that it fails because it is impossible to prove that the
decisive event of liberation for blacks has taken place. Jones requires

a *Deus ex machina,* a miracle-working God, who will set blacks free all at once, in one "mighty act" such as the exodus of the Israelites from Egypt. Obviously, such a definitive event of black liberation has not occurred and will not occur. God does not intervene supernaturally in human affairs to bring about "definitive" or "immediate" or "total" liberation of any people or condition. The theological alternative demanded by Jones (either God intervenes supernaturally or God is not a liberating God) cannot tolerate the dialectical insight that redemption occurs and shapes of freedom appear in a not-yet-redeemed world, that liberation entails conflict, struggle, suffering, defeat, death-and-resurrection, that there are setbacks and advances in the history of freedom but never triumphal, unambiguous progress. This insight is one that is or should be shared by liberal theology.

Cone rightly refuses the alternative posed by Jones, and in this sense he demonstrates a liberal sensibility. He and others have shown that freedom has in fact been experienced, affirmed, and sung about in the black community, not only after emancipation but also before it in the days of slavery, not only in the struggle for civil rights or the black power movement but also in the period of segregation. God's liberating action is not limited to historical breakthroughs such as the end of slavery or the movement toward full human and civil rights; God can set and hold a people free even in the midst of historical oppression and reversals. Indeed, the black spirituals make it clear that Christ was experienced as present precisely in the slave community, clearing a space of freedom in the midst of bondage and brutality, and the same continued to be true for the black church as the central institution of a segregated, suffering people.

African American theology helps to teach us that there is no triumphal march of God in history, no special and privileged history of salvation, but only a plurality of partial, fragmentary, ambiguous histories of freedom. What is shaped in history are fragile syntheses of values and praxis that achieve momentary, relative victories over chaos and tyranny through a process of confrontation and compromise.[12] Such syntheses endure for a while, but eventually they break down. Temporal passage involves not only a progressive evolution of practices but also disruptive reversals. History is made up of such continuities and discontinuities, which cannot be patched into an overarching linear teleology. Not only are such teleologies indefensible from the point of view of historical reality, but also they captivate us by a totalitarian vision that diverts attention from the partial victories that are possible in the historical present and to which it is our responsibility to attend. This is not to say that Hegel was wrong in describing history as the progress of the consciousness of freedom. Advances in consciousness do occur and they cannot be rescinded. Once the freedom-genie is out of the bottle it cannot be put back. It can, however, be suppressed by reactionary practices. These insights are reinforced, I believe, by feminist theology.

3. Feminist Liberation Theologies

To select one figure as representative of the enormous diversity of feminist theologies is as unsatisfactory as such a selection is for Latin American, Asian, and African American theologies. My selection is governed partly by the question about the sense in which liberation theologies are liberal theologies and with a focus on how God is construed in the emancipatory project. For these purposes the work of one of the founders of feminist liberation theology, Rosemary Radford Ruether, serves well. Part of her agenda is both to criticize and to appropriate the liberal tradition.[13]

Ruether argues that the most ancient images of the divine, widespread in the ancient Mediterranean world and India, were female: "God/ess" is a primal matrix, the great womb in which all things, gods and humans, sky and earth, are generated. As the social role of women diminished with the advent of herding and agriculture, paired female-male deities appeared, and subsequently male deities gained ascendance. But within the biblical tradition a counterthrust to patriarchalism asserted itself. The God of Israel became known as the One who liberated his people from bondage in Egypt and brought them to a new land. This experience led initially to an egalitarian society, but after the emergence of a hierarchical, landowning class the prophets established a tradition of protest that is close to the heart of biblical religion and that was renewed and radicalized by the ministry of Jesus. Jesus universalized the protest, applying it to marginalized groups such as women who had been overlooked by the prophets. He transformed the patriarchal concept of divine fatherhood into a maternal or nurturing concept of God. By bringing about the *kenosis* (emptying) of patriarchy, Jesus revealed that the relationship to God is not that of a child to a father or of a servant to a master, but of fellow-sufferers (the crucified God and liberated humanity), and that no ultimate significance attaches to gender. What is important is a new humanity, a liberated community of sisters and brothers, Jews and Christians, friends among friends. Christic personhood continues in this community.

Thus, the two primary images of God are those of primal matrix and liberator. Ruether attempts to overcome the tension between them by arguing that the idea of God embraces both the roots of material existence and the creative potential of spirit. She avoids a hierarchical dualism between matter and spirit by understanding matter (*materia*) to have also the quality of motherhood (*mater*) and thus potentially that of spirit. Matter is essentially energy, and the most highly organized and centered energy is that of consciousness or spirit. God is the infinite center in which we find the harmonization of self and body, self and other, self and world; it is the *shalom* of our being. Conversion to this center is liberation. Human beings experience the conversion not simply as a return into a cosmic womb or an achievement of cosmic communion, although there is deep truth here that is expressed in terms of ecological sensitivity and the striving for a symbiotic harmony with nature. It is also experienced as a historical project, the envisionment and actualization of an integrative human community.

What are the characteristics of such a community and what are the prospects of its realization? Ruether suggests that it would affirm democratic participation, the equal value of all persons, and equal access to educational and work opportunities. It would dismantle sexist and class hierarchies and restore ownership and management to base communities of workers. It would be an organic community in which activities are shared and integrated, and an ecological community in which human and nonhuman systems have been harmonized. Ruether acknowledges that the most we can hope to achieve are fragmentary pieces of this vision; it eludes us as a global system because the principalities and powers are still very much in control. Small utopian experiments can serve as paradigms of what might be possible under different circumstances. In limited times and places they make the world a tolerable place in which to dwell humanly, interrupting the sway of worldly powers, constraining the sphere of their influence, and occasionally leading to structural reforms.

Thus, we are brought by a somewhat different route to the conclusion suggested by Latin American, Asian, and African American theologies, that there is no triumphal march of God in history, only a plurality of partial, fragmentary, ambiguous histories of freedom appearing (as Ruether says) in the form of "livable humane balances" that achieve a momentary liberation from disharmony and tyranny. Such a conclusion is consonant with a critical yet radical liberalism that envisions the freedom project as both a prophetic judgment on history and a goal to be striven for in history but never attained. Ruether's work, like that of most feminist theologians, is based on the tools and assumptions of liberal theology but presses it to an enlarged vision that is sensitive to issues of gender, race, class, and environment, and that is aware of its own interests and social location. Liberalism's confidence that changes in consciousness do represent an advance in the history of freedom is confirmed by the liberation theologies even as they warn that such changes often evoke determined resistance and suffer tragic setbacks.

4. The Present Situation

It is well that we learn this lesson because the situation has changed considerably since the liberation theologies first appeared on the scene. On the one hand, as Mark Lewis Taylor points out, the quest for liberation has become diverse and complex. Today it includes military dissenters, prison advocates, black reparationists, socially dispossessed peoples, immigrants, indigenous peoples, environmentalists, advocates of sexual freedom (gay, lesbian, bisexual), socialist groups, international citizen movements. Taylor describes these groups as "agents of revolutionary expectation."[14]

On the other hand, the prospects for revolutionary expectation seem more remote than ever. The advances made by the liberation theologies a generation ago in raising consciousness and changing policies have been largely reversed during the past decade. Conservative movements that formed in opposition to the cultural and political changes sought by blacks, women, gays and lesbians, and the poor of the two-thirds world have become dominant and until recently have controlled all branches of government in the United States. The attacks of 9/11 and the ensuing fear of terrorism proved to be a defining moment. As a result, we have seen the resurgence of a new American imperialism with its doctrine of preemptive war, its use of torture as a strategic policy, its disregard for civil rights, and its widespread practice of deception to gain political support.[15] What surrounds us today is, in Harold Pinter's words, "a vast tapestry of lies."[16] The lies extend not only to justifications for the invasion of Iraq and policies of torture and political suppression but also to economic, social, and environmental policy. In the name of tax cuts for the middle class, tax policy has shifted to benefit the wealthy. The result has been an enormous increase in the national debt and a growing disparity between rich and poor. As a consequence of free trade, which permits multinational corporations to outsource industrial jobs to cheap labor wherever it is to be found, wages and benefits in the United State are declining and the middle class and industrial base are eroding. The gerrymandering of congressional districts has enabled Republicans to enlarge their numbers in Congress and effectively disenfranchise minorities in many areas. Democrats have been ineffective as an opposition party ever since they acquiesced to the resolution approving the war in Iraq. (Or, at least, so it seemed to me at the time of writing; with the midterm elections of 2006 the situation may have changed to some degree.) In the culture wars the attacks on evolution, the disparaging of environmental issues, the demonizing of homosexuality, and the elimination of nearly all forms of women's reproductive rights have carried the day—all in the name of "Christian" values driven by fear, anger, and an apocalyptic ideology. Christian categories and convictions have been hijacked by the religious right and distorted into a caricature of their true meaning. A gospel of love and liberation has been converted into one of hostility and intolerance, along with the naïve (or arrogant) assumption that what the right claims is what Christians believe.

So, from the point of view of radical liberalism, the situation today is bleak. It looks as though a neoconservatism with theocratic if not neofascist overtones is destroying democracy, eroding civil and human rights, subordinating women, degrading the environment, disregarding poverty, and rewarding wealthy individuals and corporations while bankrupting the nation. At the same time it is pursuing a tragically ineffective policy in the Middle East that has exacerbated interreligious hatreds, and it is not adequately protecting against terrorism and natural disasters at home. Perhaps this picture is too bleak. Historical experience shows that when nations and governments overreach they eventually collapse from their own arrogance and blindness. Today the voice of liberal theology must be one of prophetic judgment combined with a chastened hope that the freedom project will survive this trauma in world and national history.

5. Are Liberal Theologies Truly Liberation Theologies?

Perhaps it is the weakness of liberalism as a political movement and theological perspective that has contributed to this trauma. In one respect liberation theologies have offered a profound critique of liberalism. From a liberationist perspective, liberal theology has been too preoccupied with the academic discussion of doctrines and not enough with the concrete practices of Christian faith. As a consequence it has had little impact on what people actually believe and how they act. It has not embraced a preferential option for the poor, and it has failed to analyze the social and economic structures that produce poverty, focusing instead on individual moral decisions and charitable acts.[17] James Cone and other black theologians have pointed out that the liberation of the oppressed and the realities of racial injustice have not been central to the agenda of mainstream academic liberal theology. Its leading thinkers have been blind to their own social location as privileged Euro-American whites, and they have gone about their business as usual without attending to the facts of slavery, racism, and segregation, or to the literature of black religion and black theology.[18] Similar criticisms have been brought to bear from the perspective of women, gays and lesbians, and peoples of the two-thirds world. With these criticisms the tools of liberal theology have been used to deconstruct and reorient it.

Liberal theology, so it is said, is oriented to religion's "cultured despisers" (Schleiermacher's famous expression[19]) but not to culture's "despised others."[20] It is more concerned with nonbelief than nonpersons.[21] Yes, true enough. Yet I suspect that a connection exists between religion's cultured despisers and culture's despised others, between nonbelief and nonpersonhood. A culture that despises religion and turns to worldly gratifications is also likely to despise its others—its own marginalized others and the others of alien cultures. An acceptance of religion does not necessarily guarantee a different outcome. It depends on whether the religion in question is rooted in the liberating love of God or serves as an ideology that justifies oppression and intolerance. It is at the point of making such discriminations that the theological work of liberal theology is relevant to the practices of liberation theology. The latter faces a triple threat: from secularism on the left, from political and religious fundamentalism on the right, and from disengagement in the center.

The problem is that centrist-oriented liberal theology has not done its work well enough. It has failed to raise the consciousness of a majority of Christians to the realities of racism, classism, sexism, homophobia, xenophobia, and to the truth of God's radical freedom. It has not effectively communicated the power of the gospel, which is a gospel of freedom and redemption. It has backed away from a struggle for the soul of Christianity against the illiberal distortions that abound today. Whether a rediscovery of its prophetic and, yes, evangelical roots will be sufficient for it to have a transformative impact on culture and the churches remains to be seen.

One possibility would be for liberal theology to address the liberative needs of the cultural majority in the first world. They, too, suffer, but in a different way—from consumerist values, economic insecurities, personal and family crises, addictions, the fear of terrorism, the loss of meaning, deep questions about faith. By addressing their needs honestly and helping them to think critically, liberal theology might sensitize them to the global implications of the freedom project, enabling them to see not only their own situation but that of the two-thirds world. Could it become strong enough to reverse the drift of critical-minded people away from the churches into non-belief, and the drift of the churches into fundamentalism and the acceptance of cultural prejudices?

Beyond the needs of individuals, significant structural reforms are required if the promise of democratic justice is to be achieved. The socialist alternative to capitalism failed, and a triumphant capitalism has led to excesses reminiscent of the late nineteenth and early twentieth centuries. The best policy seems to lie in a balance of public and private interests whereby society assumes a share of responsibility for the health, education, and retirement security of its citizens, redistributes some degree of wealth through a progressive tax policy, ensures fair labor practices and wages, and guarantees the civil rights of all people regardless of race, ethnicity, gender, and sexual orientation. These are not extreme measures, but they seem almost utopian in light of present realities, and they become more difficult to achieve in the context of a global market. Concerted efforts are needed to reduce the economic disparities among nations that drive the most brutal forms of capitalism.

Liberal theology might help a liberal politics regain an authentic vision of not only a just society but also of a nonimperial foreign policy. During the years following the Second World War, prophetic thinkers such as Reinhold Niebuhr and George Kennan had a significant public impact along these lines.[22] They argued that the great power of the United States should be exercised with restraint and humility: in restraint resides true strength. Their strategy vis-à-vis the Soviet Union was containment, not preemption. They believed that the means of promoting democracy abroad was not to impose it by force but to create a just and humane society at home and to provide economic and policy assistance to other parts of the world. They warned that messianic self-righteousness and unrestrained *hubris* were the greatest threats to a nation—lessons that are rooted in a theological vision of God as the One who not only seeks justice but also judges idolatrous human claims (including the claim to be an agent of God).

The United States is in the grip of a cultural-political-religious fundamentalism that is all the more dangerous because of the alliance of culture, politics, and religion. Fundamentalism rejects critical reason and empirical evidence in favor of an ideological and sometimes fanatical faith that horribly distorts the biblical and theological principles to which it appeals. It supports a politics that is driven by aggression, fear, and xenophobia, and a culture that is intolerant of diversity, minority rights, and free inquiry. Liberation from the illusion of fundamentalism—as well as from the emptiness of secularism and the ineffectiveness of moral idealism—is one of the principal challenges confronting liberal theology today.

These undertakings undoubtedly are very difficult. The odds presently are against them. But why else are we called to be liberal theologians?

Liberal Theology as Ecological Theology

The freedom project involves the liberation of nature from the destructive effects of human activities and interventions. It also puzzles about nature's own intrinsic destructiveness and wonders about the place of spirit in nature. Addressing these questions calls for a contemporary philosophy and theology of nature. Hints are found in the new cosmologies proposed by postmodern science, but, despite the richness of this literature, neither the philosophical arguments nor the theological implications have been adequately worked out.[23] What is offered is a holistic vision that sees the material and the spiritual as different aspects or dimensions of the same reality. We are told that the dominant paradigm is that of relations of energy rather than substantial entities, that forces interact in complex dynamical systems, that chance and randomness are instruments of creativity, and that the cosmic story is both comic and tragic, productive of life but pushing toward decay and death.

Ecology is one aspect of a holistic, relational cosmology. It is a study (*logos*) of how our natural or cosmic "house" (*oikos*) functions; and, as Sallie McFague suggests, it involves treating this house as a home rather than as a hotel. We take care of a house but use the conveniences of a hotel.[24] According to Thomas Berry, ecological sensibility offers a comprehensive vision of the interdependence of everything in the universe, and it returns to the sense of being sustained by a "cosmic presence" such as was found in the ancient religions.[25] It is based on a model of internal relations, which means that relations are constitutive of entities rather than being something incidental to them. Events are primary, and substantial objects are enduring patterns among changing events.[26]

The primary ethical challenge of ecology is to "liberate life,"[27] that is, to liberate it from various forces of death and destructiveness that threaten the viability of life on our planet. These include the pollution of air, water, and soil, the alteration of the chemistry of the planet, the rapid depletion of natural resources, the destruction of rain forests, the elimination of living species through the loss of habitats, the uncontrolled growth in human population, the biological manipulation of life, the ideology of unlimited economic development—on the whole, the breakdown of ecological balance and an increasingly dysfunctional relationship between nature and the human spirit. The violent forces that are a necessary part of the cosmic system take on a new destructiveness in human hands. With the advent of modern technology we must assume a share of responsibility for the fate of the Earth. Exercising this responsibility requires difficult and often unpopular political decisions because they involve sacrificing short-term advantages for long-term sustainability. But we sense that ecojustice also ultimately involves political and social justice. Human well-being cannot be sustained apart from the well-being of nature. Those who seize a disproportionate share of resources for themselves harm both the human community and the environment.

A new religious sensibility corresponds to the ecological worldview. The task of liberal theology is to develop a theology of God based on metaphors drawn from ecological sensibility: life, love, and freedom. Life is the dynamism of love, love is the interrelatedness of life, and freedom is the goal of both. God as primordial *eros* and generative freedom manifests a creativity in the world that counters the force of entropy. Entropy (meaning literally a "turn in energy") is the conversion or diffusion of energy into less productive and more disruptive forms. It appears not only in closed dynamic systems but also, I believe, in open ones, in the tendency of natural forces to devolve into rivalry and violence, to enhance disorder, to move toward death rather than life. For nature as well as humanity, it seems that differentiation under the conditions of finitude becomes rupture, separation, estrangement. The struggle for life becomes excessive, it goes beyond what is necessary for survival. We see this in cancerous growth and other diseases, gratuitous violence among animals, and the destructive forces of nature (hurricanes, tsunamis, floods, earthquakes, volcanic eruptions) that destroy existing forms of life. This is the presence of tragedy in nature, its "encroachment" or "waywardness."[28] There seems to be an ontological undertow toward disintegration and destructiveness, a "futility" that is intrinsic to finitude. The divine creativity struggles against this undertow and restrains it. God is the energy of life that generates love in the world and draws it toward freedom. God makes it possible for human and natural life to survive and even flourish against otherwise overwhelming odds. God acts redemptively in relation to nature both directly, as cosmic *eros*, and indirectly, through human beings. Our responsibility is not to add to cosmic entropy by our greedy actions but to become part of God's counterentropic force, to be agents in the liberation of natural as well as human life. Biologist Stuart Kaufmann argues that there is scientific evidence of a counterentropic force that occurs "at the edge of chaos" and that spontaneously generates order and complexity, interacting with natural selection in the evolutionary process. Thus, life is an expected emergent property of matter and energy, and humans are "at home in the universe."[29] Perhaps this force can be considered an instrumentality in nature of God's *eros*, a divine lure toward integration, complexity, and freedom.

God's relationship to nature remains a mystery for humans because we cannot enter into the interiority of nature the way that

God can. We do not know how it "feels" to be a plant or animal in relation to itself, much less to its environment and the source of its being. We do not know how God acts through natural forces (it is hard enough to know how God acts in history). We are not certain what it means to say (as the Apostle Paul does) that the creation has been subjected to futility; perhaps the meaning is simply that it is not the source of its own redemption, that its freedom remains random and at cross-purposes, that on its own it suffers and turns upon itself. The world seems to be a strange mixture of order and disorder, of creativity and entropy, of vitality and decay. But of one thing we may be certain: God does not use natural forces as punishment or retribution. The destructive waters of the flood have been transformed into the cleansing/healing waters of baptism.[30] God makes use of nature to nurture and sanctify us, not destroy us. Our fitting response is to rejoice in nature's awesome beauty and to save it from the damage we inflict on it. Of course, floods and storms continue to happen, often with devastating consequences for human and other forms of life. They are part of the free flow of forces that is intrinsic to nature. God does not manipulate these forces but is present with us in suffering love as we struggle to survive them and to align our lives with them. If we do not align ourselves but instead disrupt the balance of these forces, as through global warming, they are likely to become more destructive. Liberal theology as ecological theology calls us to be responsible stewards of the Earth. Then we might hope that the whole creation will be set free from its bondage to decay and obtain to the glorious freedom of God's children.[31]

Failure in responsible stewardship can have devastating consequences. Recent evidence indicates that the effect of greenhouse gases on global warming has been more severe and accelerated than earlier anticipated. Ironically, one of the consequences could be a new flood of biblical proportions, caused by the melting of polar ice and the Greenland icecap. If the seas rise several feet during the next century, as some projections indicate, coastal cities around the globe will be inundated. This will be a flood caused not by divine wrath but by human folly. Politicians seem incapable of taking effective action to reduce the emission of carbon into the atmosphere, and corporate and religious leaders seem largely oblivious to the threat (or dismiss the scientific evidence). In the not-too-distant future, the problem will become irreversible, and prospects for the future flourishing of life will diminish.

Ecological theology anticipates comparative theology with the insight that God's spiritual presence in nature is thematized more powerfully in religions other than Christianity. Hyo-Dong Lee suggests that if the manifestations of spirit in nature and humanity—as both natural power and rational power—are understood to be truly complementary rather than hierarchical, then the category of spirit becomes more adequate as a way of naming the thematizations of ultimate reality in other, especially Asian religions. Western theologies of the Spirit prioritize the rational and personal aspects of spirit over its natural and impersonal aspects. For Daoism just the reverse is the case. The Dao is the impersonal, generative matrix that engenders all things and confers upon them the power to be what they each are, momentarily, in a transient manner. Because the Dao is neither personal presence nor rational power but creative energy, prior to any form or name, human rational activities are regarded by Daoists as secondary embellishments that often deviate from the "way" because they are rooted in human desires and reduce nature to raw material. Thus, the spontaneous flow and generation of nature are impeded. Nature's incipient or spontaneous freedom is overrun by humanity's instrumental freedom.[32] The question for comparative theology then becomes whether a Christian theology of the Spirit can recognize the Dao as a form of spirit that provides a needed corrective to the rationalizing and instrumentalizing tendencies of Western theology. If it can do so, then it might find a balance between nature and reason, affirming their unification in the Spirit in a way that goes beyond anything that has yet been envisioned.

Liberal Theology as Comparative Theology

During the past quarter century a shift has occurred in Christian attitudes toward other religions—a move away from the traditionally exclusivist claim that Christ alone is the mediator of human salvation, through the inclusivist view that recognizes the validity of other religions but believes that they have been surpassed and should be incorporated into Christian faith (the stance of classical liberal theology), to a genuine religious pluralism that accepts a diversity of ways of salvation, declines to rank them in a graded hierarchy, and encourages dialogue between them as equals. The goal of dialogue is to expose the idolatries that are present in all religions and to draw out convergent, divergent, or complementary truths.[33]

The basis of pluralism has been much debated. Some have argued that the major religions share a common ground or ultimate point of reference that is mysterious and that can never be adequately named or conceptualized; the religions represent different paths to the same goal.[34] Others have argued that the goals of the religions are actually different and cannot be synthesized; the result is a plurality of absolutes, or at least of revelations of truth and divinity that make universal claims.[35]

Another possibility is to leave open the question of the ground of pluralism and to focus instead on concrete dialogue among religions and on the comparison of specific themes. This option has been called "comparative theology" and it was first proposed by post-liberal critics of pluralistic theologies of religions.[36] In the process of dialogue one passes over into the world of another religion, allows its symbols and stories to seep into one's imagination, and then returns to one's own religion with a better understanding of what is distinctive about it. What does not seem to be allowed is that the Christian articulation of central themes such as creation, incarnation, spirit, or freedom might actually be enlarged and enriched in such a way that a deeper understanding of them emerges from a plurality of religions than from Christianity alone. But just this possibility is implicit in a genuinely comparative theology, and as a consequence the latter is more properly the project of a radically liberal theology committed to religious pluralism than of a postliberal theology committed to some form of Christian inclusivism. It is right to focus on the comparative discussion of specific themes rather than on a priori assumptions about religions, but wrong to exclude the possibility of comparative or relational truth that transcends the truth of a particular religion.

Paul Knitter, in his critique of postliberal versions of comparative theology, makes several points.[37]

(a) While it is true that the language of a specific religion serves as a *prism* for all that we see and do, it need not also be a *prison*. If it is not to remain isolated and fideistic, the prism must be open to wider refractions. It is in fact possible, as many people have demonstrated, to be religiously bilingual and to experience a multiple belonging, a belonging in which the truth of more than one faith is affirmed.

(b) To insist on the incompatibility of multiple salvations limits the possibility of what can happen in actual dialogical relationships. Among religions there are not simply differences but also commonalities, which do not necessarily exist in advance but appear with the challenges of the real world: injustice, violence, ecological devastation. Suffering may be the material from which common ground is fashioned and on which a global ethic of solidarity is based.

(c) "Absolute" indicates a particular truth that is universally taught, and a plurality of absolutes can be affirmed without having to grade them. Since the absolute can never be known absolutely, we can learn from a diversity of absolute claims. The existence of many absolutes does not mean that there is no absolute but rather that absolutes are in need of each other and have to connect in dialogue—a complementarity of absolutes, not an identity. Religions may be like galaxies of the universe, none of which occupies the center; rather, there is a multiplicity of centers that together comprise a plural whole.

(d) It is naïve to think that comparative theology can bracket certain theological assumptions. The question about claims that Christ is the only source of salvation for all of humanity cannot be deferred endlessly, as the postliberal comparativists desire. Now is the time to acknowledge that such claims are incompatible with a genuinely comparative theology, which brings with it the recognition that the revelation of salvific wisdom transcends and enriches Christ, and also that faith in Christ opens his followers to truth wherever and however it appears.

Another analysis of interreligious dialogue and comparative theology has been articulated by Hyo-Dong Lee.[38] He argues that the critiques of a pluralistic theology of religions from postliberal and neoconservative perspectives fail to take into account the postcolonial context of today's religious plurality, and that they set forth an alternative colonization based on claims of Christian superiority. Against this view Lee turns to Hegel's idea of free and uncoerced reciprocal recognition in which each party grants freedom to the other. To guard against a spurious, condescending recognition that does not accept a parity of values, Lee argues that a solidary interreligious relationship also requires recognition of an equality of worth. Hegel shows that in the recognitive process my initial totalizing horizon undergoes a transformation when it encounters the other as the voice of the infinite that cannot simply be "my" other. There ensues a journey of self-transformative encounter with the other's self-disclosure. In the realm of interreligious dialogue this is the role played by a comparative theological engagement with the other's depth of riches. A dialectic occurs between the infinity of the other and the relative totality of my own religious perspective, leading to a new and expanded theological horizon. The dialectic spirals ahead into either the discovery of irreconcilable differences or the coalescence of a pattern of mutual compatibility and complementarity. In either case the colonization created by hierarchical binary oppositions is overcome: the differences are honored or the compatibility is celebrated. Instead of returning to an originary myth of homogeneity, comparative theology must be a political act of solidarity with suppressed subaltern voices of difference, a solidarity that achieves participatory parity. In this parity a coalescence may occur that produces a new, interreligiously hybrid narrative. If it does not, there persists a mutual recognition and acceptance of different narratives.

Comparative theology pursued along the lines suggested by Knitter and Lee will have a liberating effect. I have made a brief attempt at such a theology with a focus on the theme of the Spirit.[39] Starting from a Christian point of view, I assume that God has something to do with the fact that a diversity of independent ways of salvation appears in the history of the world. This diversity reflects the diversity or plurality within the divine life itself, of which the doctrine of the Trinity provides an account (an account that emerges from the narrative of Christian experience). The mystery of the Trinity is for Christians the ultimate foundation of pluralism. Within this mystery Christ introduces a principle of determinateness, of God's concrete incarnation in a specific human being, while the Spirit introduces a principle of universality, the wholeness from which the Spirit proceeds as God returns to godself from creating, indwelling, and redeeming the world. The Spirit proceeds not just from Christ but from the whole world, from a diversity of religious figures and traditions as well as from diverse natural powers. Thus, we cannot say exhaustively what the Spirit is: Spirit is both concretely configured (in Christ and other figures) and open to new possibilities. The difference between Christ and the Spirit is not, in my view, the difference between two distinct hypostases in the Godhead, but the difference between God's concrete historical presence and universal indwelling power, between fixity and fluidity, history and mysticism, incarnation and communion. Both are necessary to the religion of the concrete Spirit,[40] which is a religion of freedom—God's radical freedom, nature's incipient freedom, and humanity's liberated freedom.

The Spirit is moving through the great religious traditions. It has always been so, but today communication, travel, and research bring these traditions together as never before. We now have a far richer and more accurate sense of the diversity of religious manifestations from which the Spirit proceeds. God does not tightly control the particulars of this procession, which depends in part on the contingencies of the world, but we have reason to believe that God creates the world, becomes incarnate in Christ and other savior figures, and sends the Spirit toward an end—an end that can never be fully grasped but includes such goals as an enhancement of life and diversity, a harmonious dwelling together of the whole cosmos, a struggle to heal tragic conflicts, a growth in love and freedom, enlightenment and wisdom, goodness and beauty. The reason for believing this is that such goals and values are affirmed, often in strikingly different ways, by the great religions and cultures of the world. A few deep and enduring values have emerged from the refinery of history, despite the recalcitrance and self-centeredness of human beings, and we can take this as proof that God's Spirit has been at work in the great cultural trajectories. These values are often distorted by the interests that produced them, and in every culture outright contradictions and ambiguities occur. The special challenge today is to keep the refining process going by encouraging religions, through dialogue and interaction, to identify one another's blind spots and to contribute reciprocally to the spiritual growth of all. The outcome will not be a melding of religions but a deepened insight into each tradition and a sharing of resources toward the end of mutual enrichment and transformation.

The Holy Spirit provides a window for Christians onto the diversity and plurality of world religions. A theology of the Spirit is a Christian way of construing this diversity and plurality, relating it to the purposes, activity, and being of God. It is only one such construal, and it must accept that other religions interpret the diversity differently. It has no monopoly on the truth. If faith in the Spirit of Jesus Christ means openness to truth wherever it manifests itself, Christians should have no fear of entering into the dialogical process, offering their own deep insights and eager to learn from others.

A theology of religions seems to have a twofold task, one critical and the other constructive: exposing idolatries and drawing out convergent, divergent, and complementary truths. The Spirit is at work in both of these tasks as a "refining fire" that burns away the evil present in all religions and as an "attracting wind" that draws the religions into mutually enriching dialogue and practices. Where the Spirit is leading on this adventure no one knows. I do not believe it is toward a monolithic world religion but rather toward the discovery of a liberative and compassionate core of spiritual wisdom present in all the great religious traditions. I believe there can and will be a heightened appreciation of both plurality and solidarity among the religions. Solidarity arises through a mutually correcting coalescence of diverse interests and insights rather than by the imposition of totalitarian claims. The plurality will frequently remain recalcitrant, resistant to easy unification; and when solidarity is achieved under such conditions it is a spiritual gift.

As a brief example of comparative theology, I shall look at how spirit concresces in the two great India-born religions, Hinduism and Buddhism. I have no expertise in this subject and rely on secondary studies.[41] My interest is in what a Christian theology of the Spirit might learn from the depth of their riches.[42] Brahman/Atman, the ultimate reality for Hinduism, is understood to be a generative spiritual matrix. "Through a process that is inexplicable, this universal ultimate reality became subdivided into myriad individual atmans [spirits]. They are the truly real entities in the world. . . . All beings, then, are spiritual beings, sharing with one another and the forces that move the universe a common spiritual essence."[43] Brahman is both impersonal and personal. As the underlying substance of things it is impersonal, but as the original and true self it goes out from itself, creates gods, other selves, a world that keeps evolving, becoming more complex. Everything interacts in the spiritual nexus. As an individual self I am implicitly identical with the universal self, and my spiritual journey is to find my way back to the original interconnectedness of things, reversing the process of creation whereby the original self becomes many. The one is many and the many are one: Advaita Vedanta (one of the Hindu schools) grasps the nonidentity and nonduality of things more subtly than most Western philosophy does. It reflects the Hegelian vision of spirit as the unity of substance and subject and as a nontotalizing wholeness. It holds together the two central attributes of divinity, impersonal power and personal presence, without dissolving the tension between them or the mystery of their connection.

The personal aspect of spirit appears in a multitude of Hindu divinities. Brahma, though a relatively minor figure in ritual practice, is the creator of gods and mortals, and a wise counselor. In Vishnu,

God comes down to earth and is present in many incarnations of which Krishna is the most complex and multifaceted, appearing in diverse human forms from infant to guru. Shiva, by contrast, represents the transcendent, unpredictable, creative-destructive aspect of divinity, symbolized as sexual yet spiritual. The function of these divinities is to manifest the inexhaustible complexity of Brahman-Spirit in forms that humans can grasp and with which they can interact. Intellectual knowledge is not enough: the truth must be realized through ascetic practices (yoga), which achieve a progressive sensing of the spirit within and a reversing of ignorance and egoistic desire.

The goddess figure, Mahadevi, combines and unifies the several functions of the male divinities more completely than they themselves do. In this respect she is closer to Brahman, the unmanifested Spirit. She represents the materialization of spiritual energy—a materialization that is necessary if the Spirit is to proceed from the interaction of God and the world, the immaterial and the material, the ideal and the real. The goddess appears as Kali, the Great Mother, the consort of Shiva, combining violent power and gentle protection; she is the source of death and destruction on the one hand, and of strength and justice on the other. As such she reflects the role played by women in primitive matriarchies as well as the respect and fear of female power. What is the significance of having a goddess figure at the heart of a religion that is deeply patriarchal in tradition and practice? Does she point to an egalitarian and liberating core, to the fact that, if all things have their being within Brahman, then all distinctions and hierarchies, including spirit and nature, male and female, brahmin and outcast, are opposed to the Advaitic Spirit?

Hinduism portrays the unity and diversity of what we call spirit more dramatically and colorfully than anything known in the West. Compressed into Brahman, spirit then explodes into a pandemonium of divinities. Contrasts and paradoxes are heightened, but they prove ultimately not to be paradoxes since they lie beyond dualistic logic. Hinduism is overwhelming in its wild and sensuous variety, its celebration of raw spiritual power. Because of its internal pluralism, it is tolerant of other religions and is capable of subsuming them within its own mythic structures. Sharp tensions are evident between its core philosophical insights and its social practices insofar as they legitimate class hierarchies, encourage extreme forms of asceticism, and perpetuate the subordination of women. From a Western Christian post-Enlightenment perspective, legitimate concerns can be raised about Hinduism as it struggles with the challenges of modernity and postmodernity. But we also have much to learn from its ancient wisdom. The Spirit that concresces in the gods, goddesses, myths, philosophies, rituals, and practices of Hinduism is like a whirlwind that shakes and disturbs the settled spiritualities of our own religion, reminding us that the Spirit blows where and how it will.

Buddhism represents a reform and simplification of the old Vedic religion from which both Hinduism and it emerged. It is often said to be a nontheistic religion, and if this is true, how can it be called a religion of the Spirit? Brahman disappears as a thematized concept and is replaced by Nirvana as its negative counterpart. Nirvana refers to the "cooling" of feverish desires that create *karma* and bind individuals into *samsara,* the world of rebirth and suffering. It means "freedom and existence in an eternal state beyond all material description." Human beings can realize Nirvana by the cultivation of insight or wisdom (*prajna*), by appropriate moral practices, and by proper meditation. The way to Nirvana is established by the Four Noble Truths and the Eightfold Path attributed to the Buddha (Gautama Siddhartha). Accompanying the concept of Nirvana is that of the "nonself," which rejects the idea of "an essential, unchanging interior entity at the center of a person"—the soul or *atman* of Hinduism. Human beings are subject to the law of impermanence and are simply a continuously changing, interdependent relationship among five aggregates: the physical body, feelings, perceptions, mental dispositions, and consciousness.[44] Despite the rejection of the substantial soul, Buddhism does not reject, as far as I can tell, the Hindu conviction of a universal spiritual matrix in which everything subsists. Nirvana is the purest form of this matrix.

Westerners have found deep spiritual wisdom in the teaching and practices of Buddhism. Gautama, John Cobb points out,[45] taught that we suffer because we are attached to things, and that when we relinquish this attachment we become free. The result is a freedom for all things because it is a complete freedom from all things. This detachment is more radical than anything known in the West: it is both a total emptiness and a total fullness. Christian spirituality approximates this sense of total detachment, but it is hindered by a cultural heritage of possession, ownership, self-activity, and individual fulfillment. What Buddhists call detachment, Christians call "grace," a term that refers to the empowering power of the Holy Spirit, the sanctifying gift of wisdom, compassion, and freedom. Living by grace entails a complete letting go, not a holding fast, an openness to what presents itself in experience, a gaining of life by losing it. Such grace is the basic condition and constitutive reality of the church as a spiritual community, which is a community of compassion, freedom, communion with and for the other. Such a community is a utopian ideal in our consumer-oriented, materialist, individualist culture. Buddhism can help the Christian church to be a community of grace in a graceless culture by showing more clearly what it means to have faith without attachment, to find fulfillment in emptiness, to become a communal self by giving up private selfhood. Conversely, questions can be raised from a Christian perspective about the relative failure of Buddhism to develop an ethic of social transformation that corresponds to its vision of compassion and freedom, although Buddhist scholars such as Masao Abe[46] have argued for a dynamic interpretation of Nirvana (Sunyata) that might yield such an ethic. In any event, dialogue with Christians can help Buddhists move in this direction.

Perhaps the central issue between Christians and Buddhists is whether humans need a source of strength outside themselves to break the power of ego. Is it is a question of other-power or of self-power? Christian trust in grace and the Holy Spirit clearly indicates that the source comes from outside ourselves, although the empowering power of the Spirit works within the self as well as in history and culture. If Buddhism is a nontheistic religion, it might seem that enlightenment comes solely from our own disciplined efforts,[47] although it is somewhat ironic to speak of self-power in the context of a doctrine of the nonself. Rather, for Buddhism it may be more a matter of connecting oneself with the universal *dharma,* the path of truthful teaching and enlightenment that functions rather like grace and has a numinous, sacred aspect. Taitetsu Unno quotes William James to the effect that what is involved in Buddhism is "not a deity *in concreto,* not a superhuman person, but the immanent divinity in things, the essentially spiritual structure of the universe." He goes on to say that the embodiment of *dharma* in the Buddha "is central to the radical self-sufficiency found in the [Buddha's] injunction, 'Be ye lamps unto yourselves.' The self here is not the unenlightened ego self, but the enlightened non-ego self imbued with *dharma,* as clearly understood in the subsequent passage, 'Hold fast to the *dharma* as a lamp. Seek salvation alone in the *dharma.*'"[48]

This lamp, for Jews and Christians, is the light of the Holy Spirit. "Your word [O Lord] is a lamp to my feet and a light to my path" (Psalm 119:105). Here Buddhism, Judaism, and Christianity share deep spiritual insight. For Judaism the *dharma* is the Torah, while for Christianity it is the teaching not just of Jesus but of the cumulative wisdom of Judaism and the saints and theologians of the church. Can we Christians share with Buddhists the injunction, "Rely on the teaching and not the teacher"?[49] But if the teaching is completely realized in a teacher, as is believed to be the case with both the Buddha and Jesus, then the teacher and the teaching, while distinguishable, are inseparable. The teacher is the concrete proclaimer and performer of the teaching. The teaching itself is the gift of the Spirit, or more directly, the teaching *is* the Spirit.

In today's complex, interconnected, and conflicted world we need not only the Torah and the Gospel but also the *dharma*; not only Christ but also Buddha; not only the one personal Spirit of Christianity but also the impersonality of Brahman and the multiple spirits of Hinduism. We need these resources as we struggle to comprehend the mystery of God as the One who is radically free and who sets the whole creation free from its bondage to decay and evil. We discover that Hinduism and Buddhism are religions of freedom and of spirit. We learn that freedom is a more complex, multifaceted reality than anything we have experienced in the West. This detracts not at all from the depth of riches of Judaism and Christianity, or the great

insights of Western philosophy, or the advances of the Enlightenment. Freedom is a work in progress, and it will be reshaped as a
diversity of religiocultural trajectories cross paths in the years ahead.

An Unfinished Conclusion

At the end of this project I am aware of its limitations. I have
given only a sketch of current theological options. I have turned to a
thinker of the nineteenth century to address contested issues facing
the twenty-first century, and I have not engaged many of the contemporary voices of postmodernity. My discussion of complex matters
related to liberation, ecology, and pluralism focuses on a few themes.
I have not considered personal aspects of sin, evil, and suffering and
what redemption from conditions caused by them might entail.[50]
Nor have I considered the terrible distortions of freedom that darken
the pages of history.[51] My work is one example of a liberal theology
for today, not a definitive statement. The task is unfinished—indeed,
it is just beginning—and so the conclusion must be unfinished. I
simply write the following.

Liberal theology is radicalized, driven to its roots, when it
confronts the contested sites of postmodernity with its mediating
imagination, when it engages in the emancipatory struggles of our
time, when it expands its horizon to encompass the ecology of nature,
and when it opens itself to the redemptive power that is present in
other religions. At the roots it reconstructs the enduring themes
of Christian theology and discovers the freedom project, which is
simply God's saving presence in the world. Here it encounters the
mystery beneath the real.

Liberal theology has been under attack partly for its perceived
failings and partly because the cultural mood has shifted. More than
ever today its critical and prophetic voice is needed to counter the
forces of superstition and intolerance on one side and cynicism and
nihilism on the other. I write with a sense of urgency. The political,
cultural, and environmental problems that we face today are deadly

serious, life threatening. Under these circumstances the delusional character of the dominant religiosity of our time, and of the policies it supports, is extremely dangerous. The virulent antiliberalism that pervades much of the cultural and political environment threatens the future of liberal democracy as we know it.[52] In the face of these threats, bold thought and courageous action are required. I believe that liberal theology has a future if it does not shrink from the enormous theological and ethical challenges of the twenty-first century. It brings the resources of a great tradition to bear on these challenges, but it must not be a prisoner of its past. It has to face forward with daring—with the determination to reinvent itself from time to time. I am a product of a phase of the history of liberal theology that is now past. I offer to the next generation of theologians the little that I have learned, in hopes that the radical vision will shine brightly in their works.

Acknowledgments

THE AUTHOR EXPRESSES APPRECIATION FOR permission to make use of materials he has published previously:

From *The Future of Liberal Theology*, edited by Mark D. Chapman. Copyright © 2002 Mark D. Chapman. Used by permission of Ashgate Publishing.

From *The Myth of Religious Superiority: Multifaith Explorations of Religious Pluralism*, edited by Paul F. Knitter. Copyright © 2005 Paul F. Knitter. Used by permission of Orbis Books.

From *Hegel and Christian Theology: A Reading of the Lectures on the Philosophy of Religion*, by Peter C. Hodgson. Copyright © 2005 Peter C. Hodgson. Used by permission of Oxford University Press.

From *Winds of the Spirit: A Constructive Christian Theology*, by Peter C. Hodgson. Copyright © 1994 Peter C. Hodgson. Used by permission of Westminster John Knox Press.

Notes

Chapter 1

1. Paul Lakeland, *Postmodernity: Christian Identity in a Fragmented Age*, Guides to Theological Inquiry (Minneapolis: Fortress Press, 1997), 1–11.

2. Elaine Graham, "Liberal Theology and Transformative Pedagogy: A Response to Peter Hodgson," in *The Future of Liberal Theology*, ed. Mark D. Chapman (Aldershot, U.K. and Burlington, Vt.: Ashgate Publishing, 2002), 129–38 (quotations from 138). In this chapter I draw at various points upon my essay to which she is responding, "Liberal Theology and Transformative Pedagogy," 99–128. Used by permission of Ashgate. This book contains materials presented at a conference, "The Future of Christian Theology—the Contribution of Liberal Traditions," held at the University of York, U.K., in March 1999.

3. Gary Dorrien points this out in *The Making of American Liberal Theology*, vol. 3: *Crisis, Irony, and Postmodernity*, 1950–2005 (Louisville: Westminster John Knox Press, 2006). This volume was published too recently to be taken into account in the present book.

4. Eberhard Busch, *Karl Barth: His Life from Letters and Autobiographical Texts*, trans. John Bowden (Philadelphia: Fortress Press, 1976), 81.

5. See Mark Chapman's description of these criticisms in his introduction to *The Future of Liberal Theology*, 6–13.

6. Lakeland, *Postmodernity*, 10–16.

7. Mark C. Taylor, *Erring: A Postmodern A/theology* (Chicago: University of Chicago Press, 1984), 7–8.

8. Lakeland, *Postmodernity*, 10–18, 39–45.

9. Niebuhr met with small groups of students for conversation at dinner. My memory of a conversation in February 1959, in which he said this about Barth and described himself as "postliberal," is refreshed by a letter that I wrote at the time and that is still in my possession.

10. H. Richard Niebuhr, "Next Steps in Theology" (The Cole Lectures, 1961), in *Theology, History, and Culture: Major Unpublished Writings,* ed. William Stacy Johnson (New Haven: Yale University Press, 1996), 3–18. In a considerably earlier lecture contained in this volume, "Theology in a Time of Disillusionment" (1931), as well as in other writings from the 1930s and 1940s, Niebuhr was much more critical of liberal theology, concluding that it was passing away (xxvii, 110–16). As far as I know, he did not use the term *postliberal* in his writings. He did not like labels. He (like his brother Reinhold) is better described as a "neoliberal."

11. George Lindbeck, *The Nature of Doctrine* (Philadelphia: Westminster Press, 1984), quotation from 118; Lakeland, *Postmodernity,* 64–66.

12. Hans W. Frei, *The Eclipse of Biblical Narrative* (New Haven: Yale University Press, 1974); *The Identity of Jesus Christ* (Philadelphia: Fortress Press, 1975); and *Types of Christian Theology,* ed. George Hunsinger and William C. Placher (New Haven: Yale University Press, 1992).

13. This is evident from his brilliant, detailed study of Richard Niebuhr's theological background in *Faith and Ethics: The Theology of H. Richard Niebuhr,* ed. Paul Ramsey (New York: Harper & Brothers, 1957), 9–64.

14. Kathryn Tanner, *Theories of Culture: A New Agenda for Theology,* Guides to Theological Inquiry (Minneapolis: Fortress Press, 1997), 38–57, 64–65, 114–16, 135–36, 144–51.

15. See below, pp. 52–58.

16. Introduction to *Radical Orthodoxy: A New Theology,* ed. John Milbank, Catherine Pickstock, and Graham Ward (London and New York: Routledge, 1999), esp. 1–4.

17. Chapman, introduction, *The Future of Liberal Theology,* 10–11.

18. Lakeland, *Postmodernity,* 68–75.

19. Michael Langford, *A Liberal Theology for the Twenty-First Century: A Passion for Reason* (Aldershot, U.K. and Burlington, Vt.: Ashgate Publishing, 2001), chap. 1.

20. See *The Spire* (published by Vanderbilt University Divinity School) 24, no. 1 (Fall 2003): 16.

21. H. Richard Niebuhr, *Christ and Culture* (New York: Harper & Brothers, 1951), 239. Maurice in turn was following John Stuart Mill. This dictum can be turned against Niebuhr's own critiques of liberal theology.

22. For example, according to Daniel Day Williams, Reinhold Niebuhr, when pressed, could not identify a single thinker who actually fitted the monstrous system of liberal ideas he conjured up in his book *Christian Realism and Political Problems* (New York: Scribner's, 1953). See L. Harold DeWolf, *The Case for Theology in Liberal Perspective* (Philadelphia: Westminster Press, 1959), 11–13. Gary Dorrien points out that both Reinhold and Richard Niebuhr distorted liberal theology in their critiques, yet remained deeply under its influence and late in their careers found qualified ways of reaffirming it. See *The Making of American Liberal Theology*, vol. 2: *Idealism, Realism, and Modernity, 1900–1950* (Louisville: Westminster John Knox Press, 2003), chaps. 7 (esp. 477–83), 8.

23. Quoted by Peter Baelz in D. W. Hardy and P. H. Sedgwick, eds., *The Weight of Glory: A Vision and Practice for Christian Faith: The Future of Liberal Theology: Essays for Peter Baelz* (Edinburgh: T & T Clark, 1991), 15.

24. Niebuhr, *Theology, History, and Culture*, 6–8.

25. *The Making of American Liberal Theology*, vol. 1: *Imagining Progressive Religion, 1805–1900* (Louisville: Westminster John Knox Press, 2001), xiii.

26. The Consultation will meet over several years and has a Web site at Harvard (http://isites.harvard.edu/k2446) through which copies of papers can be obtained. (Registration is required to use the site.)

27. Mark Lewis Taylor, *Religion, Politics, and the Christian Right: Post–9/11 Powers and American Empire* (Minneapolis: Fortress Press, 2005), chaps. 4, 7.

28. See Claude Welch's careful accounting in *Protestant Thought in the Nineteenth Century*, 2 vols. (New Haven: Yale University Press, 1972, 1985), 2:221–38.

29. See my discussion of Troeltsch in *God in History: Shapes of Freedom* (Nashville: Abingdon Press, 1989), 130–47.

30. Reading through Gary Dorrien's *The Making of American Liberal Theology* reminds me how much of the American liberal tradition was

neglected in my own theological formation—starting with the Unitarians and transcendentalists at the beginning of the nineteenth century (William Ellery Channing, Ralph Waldo Emerson, Theodore Parker), then the singular genius of Horace Bushnell and the leaders of reform at midcentury (Henry Ward Beecher, Elizabeth Cady Stanton), on through the academic liberals (Charles A. Briggs, Borden Parker Bowne, William Adams Brown) and the social gospelers (Washington Gladden, Walter Rauschenbusch, Vida Scudder) at the turn of the century, to the twentieth-century Boston personalists (Albert Knudson, Edgar Brightman) and Chicago empiricists and pragmatists (G. B. Foster, Shailer Mathews, D. C. Macintosh, Henry Nelson Wieman). Nor am I as well informed as I would like on the important trajectory of British liberalism from Charles Gore to William Temple and F. R. Tennant, Ian Ramsey, Charles Raven, Alec Vidler, John Hick, Maurice Wiles. I studied some of these thinkers (principally Bushnell), but not the whole systematically. My orientation has been more to the German tradition. However, Friedrich Wilhelm Graf's article, "What Has London (or Oxford or Cambridge) to Do with Augsburg: The Enduring Significance of the German Liberal Tradition in Christian Theology," in Chapman, ed., *The Future of Liberal Theology*, 18–38, shows that German liberalism had a complicated history filled with contradictions and paradoxes.

31. Dorrien, *The Making of American Liberal Theology*, 1:xix. The reference is to Daniel Day Williams, *God's Grace and Man's Hope* (New York: Harper & Brothers, 1949), 22.

32. Dorrien, 1:xxi–xxiii.

33. Ernst Troeltsch, "Religion and the Science of Religion" (1906), in Robert Morgan and Michael Pye, trans. and ed., *Ernst Troeltsch: Writings on Theology and Religion* (Louisville: Westminster John Knox Press, 1990), 119–20. The expression "free theology" (*die freie Theologie*) was already used by Alois Emanuel Biedermann in his early work, *Die Freie Theologie oder Philosophie und Christentum im Streit und Frieden* (Tübingen, 1844), in which he argued that the challenge to theology posed in particular by David Friedrich Strauss and Ludwig Feuerbach concerned the truth or falsity of Christianity as a whole. Biedermann defended its truth in his *Christliche Dogmatik* (Zürich, 1869; 2nd ed., 1884–85) on the basis of a free rational critique of its dogmatic forms and a disci-

plined "scientific" reconstruction that would utilize philosophy without reducing religion to it. The "principle of Christianity" is that of redemption and childhood to God based on the unity of God and humanity in Christ. It leads to the absolute freedom of the human spirit. Claude Welch, ed. and trans., *God and Incarnation in Mid-Nineteenth Century German Theology* (New York: Oxford University Press, 1965), 288–93, 311, 366–72.

34. Martha C. Nussbaum, *Cultivating Humanity: A Classical Defense of Reform in Liberal Education* (Cambridge, Mass.: Harvard University Press, 1997), 30–35, 293–300.

35. On the pedagogical implications, see my book *God's Wisdom: Toward a Theology of Education* (Louisville: Westminster John Knox Press, 1999).

36. This is the central theme of Horace Bushnell's *Christian Nurture,* first published in 1848. The most recent edition is by Pilgrim Press (Cleveland, 1994). See Hodgson, *God's Wisdom,* 35–39. Bushnell and other liberal theologians (e.g., Schleiermacher and Biedermann) made good use of the image of divine childhood.

37. It was in this negative sense that the expression *theologia liberalis* was first used in the eighteenth century by the German church historian Johann Salomo Semler to describe a purely historical investigation of the Bible and tradition unconstrained by dogmatic presuppositions. Later in Germany it became associated with a program of practical and rational Christianity, and then with a post-Christian religion of humanity, all of which gave it a negative connotation and made it the target of orthodox attacks. See Graf, "What Has London (or Oxford or Cambridge) to Do with Augsburg," *The Future of Liberal Theology*, 25–27.

38. The *Oxford Encyclopedic English Dictionary* defines "liberal" as "giving freely, generous, not sparing; open-minded, not prejudiced; not literal (of interpretation); for general broadening of the mind." The negative aspect of "liberal" is described as "regarding many traditional beliefs as dispensable, invalidated by modern thought, or liable to change." See Dorrien, *The Making of American Liberal Theology,* 1:xix. I find the negative definition somewhat misleading: it is not so much that traditional beliefs are dispensable as it is that they must be critically evaluated and rethought.

39. Openness includes, of course, the possibility of criticism and protest.

40. This phrase comes from John Habgood, "Reflection on the Liberal Position," in Hardy and Sedgwick, *The Weight of Glory,* 12. He writes that, while there is no "identikit" for being a liberal, it is possible to recognize "some whose lives have clearly been shaped by the gracious liberality of God, and who display its marks in their own liberality toward all that God has made."

41. Andrew Shanks, *Faith in Honesty: The Essential Nature of Theology* (Aldershot, U.K. and Burlington, Vt.: Ashgate Publishing, 2005), esp. 1–13.

42. Ferdinand Christian Baur, Adolf Harnack, and Ernst Troeltsch were the great historical-critical theologians of Protestant liberalism.

43. Immanuel Kant's watchword for the Enlightenment was *sapere aude!* ("think boldly!"), and he was the author of the great critiques of theoretical, practical, and aesthetic reason.

44. It was the fear of indifference or indulgence that led Bushnell to avoid the word *liberal,* which he construed in purely negative terms, and to propose instead a "comprehensive" theology. See the essay "Christian Comprehensiveness," in *Horace Bushnell,* ed. H. Shelton Smith (New York: Oxford University Press, 1965), 106–26.

45. An example of this is the failure of the mainstream theological tradition, from the beginning right through the liberal theologians of the nineteenth and early twentieth centuries, to recognize injustice based on gender, race, and class. But this does not invalidate the enormous struggle for truth that has gone on in the tradition.

46. Peter C. Hodgson, *Winds of the Spirit: A Constructive Christian Theology* (Louisville: Westminster John Knox Press, 1994), chaps. 1, 3, 4.

47. Niebuhr, *Theology, History, and Culture,* 19–33.

48. For an excellent study, see Wayne Proudfoot, *Religious Experience* (Berkeley and Los Angeles: University of California Press, 1985). Hegel argued that *knowledge* is the matrix in which religion occurs. But he understood experience in the form of religious feeling to be a form of knowledge—a sense-based form that must be taken up into higher representational and reflective forms. He differed from Schleiermacher in understand-

ing Christianity to involve the experience not of utter dependence but of absolute freedom. G. W. F. Hegel, *Lectures on the Philosophy of Religion,* ed. and trans. Peter C. Hodgson, et al. (Berkeley and Los Angeles: University of California Press, 1984–87; reprint, Oxford: Oxford University Press, 2007), 1:380–413, 3:171–72; Peter C. Hodgson, *Hegel and Christian Theology: A Reading of the Lectures on the Philosophy of Religion* (Oxford: Oxford University Press, 2005), 46–47, 64–66, 96–97, 108–11.

49. Nancey Murphy, *Beyond Liberalism and Fundamentalism* (Valley Forge, Pa.: Trinity Press International, 1996), chap. 1.

50. Hodgson, *Winds of the Spirit,* chaps. 1–2.

51. Niebuhr, *Theology, History, and Culture,* 34–49.

52. Friedrich Schleiermacher, *The Christian Faith,* ed. H. R. Macintosh and J. S. Stewart (Edinburgh: T & T Clark, 1928), § 4.

53. Ibid., §§ 11, 29.

54. See Paul Rasor's discussion of "religious experience and language" in *Faith without Certainty: Liberal Theology in the 21st Century* (Boston: Skinner House Books, 2005), 109–40.

55. Schleiermacher, *The Christian Faith,* §§ 15, 28.

56. Troeltsch, "Religion and the Science of Religion," in *Writings on Theology and Religion,* 82–123.

57. Hodgson, *God's Wisdom,* 132–35.

58. Ernst Troeltsch, *The Christian Faith (Glaubenslehre),* Fortress Texts in Modern Theology, trans. Garrett E. Paul (Minneapolis: Fortress Press, 1991), 73–84, 195–204.

59. This phrase is suggested by the Victorian novelist George Eliot, whose realist fiction is suffused by religious themes. See my book, *The Mystery beneath the Real: Theology in the Fiction of George Eliot* (London: SCM Press; and Minneapolis: Fortress Press, 2001).

60. On this way of reading Hegel, see Cyril O'Regan, *The Heterodox Hegel* (Albany: State University of New York Press, 1994) (O'Regan attends especially to Hegel's stance in the mystical tradition and to his speculative metanarrative); Robert R. Williams, *Recognition: Fichte and Hegel on the Other* (Albany: State University of New York Press, 1992), esp.

chap. 11 on Hegel's holism; and my book, *Hegel and Christian Theology.* See also chap. 2 below.

61. Murphy, *Beyond Liberalism and Fundamentalism,* chaps. 4–5. Murphy also calls for a metaphysical holism in chap. 6, but what she offers there, drawing upon some postmodern cosmologies and philosophies of science, seems impoverished by comparison with the philosophical wealth of Hegel or Whitehead.

62. Raimon Panikkar, *The Cosmotheandric Experience* (Maryknoll, N.Y.: Orbis Books, 1993).

63. Ernst Troeltsch, "The Ethics of Cultural Values," in *Christian Thought: Its History and Application,* ed. Baron F. von Hügel (London: University of London Press, 1923), 69–99. For his general cultural assessment just before his death in 1923, see the whole of sections 2 and 3 of this book, which contains lectures he was to have delivered in England.

64. Troeltsch, *The Christian Faith,* 174–94, 204–23, 253–59.

65. In our current situation I am struck by Niebuhr's warning that a newly assertive American empire might be tempted to engage in "preventive war." Reinhold Niebuhr, *The Irony of American History* (New York: Charles Scribner's Sons, 1952), 146. I acquired this book in 1954, while in college, and was deeply moved by it as well as by Niebuhr's other writings of the 1950s and by Paul Tillich's *The Protestant Era,* which I read a year earlier. The influence of Niebuhr and Tillich preceded my encounter with Karl Barth, and they together with him modified my later path to liberalism. They helped to make me a radical liberal.

66. Paul Tillich, *The Protestant Era,* trans. James Luther Adams (Chicago: University of Chicago Press, 1948), 163.

67. H. Richard Niebuhr, *Christ and Culture,* chap. 6. See below, chap. 2.

68. Hodgson, *Winds of the Spirit,* chaps. 5–8. I take up the same themes in chap. 3, below.

69. Paul Tillich's *Systematic Theology,* 3 vols. (Chicago: University of Chicago Press, 1951–63), is the definitive example of a theology of correlation. The five parts of his system correlate reason and revelation, being and God, existence and the Christ, life and the Spirit, history and the kingdom of God.

70. Presentation to the American Academy of Religion Consultation on Liberal Theologies, November 2005.

71. See above, n. 26.

72. Marilyn McCord Adams makes a similar point in different terms. As she puts it, "God is very, very big and we are very, very small." For her, too, liberal theology is rooted in the gracious liberality of God, a liberality that transcends all limited human claims and narrow doctrinal formulations. Her identification of fundamental convictions about God and human nature that are shared by liberals is quite helpful in the context of struggles that are currently roiling the Anglican Communion and other churches. See "A Shameless Defense of a Liberal Church," *Modern Believing: Church and Society*, 48:1 (Jan. 2007), 25-37.

73. Thus the NRSV. The RSV, following the KJV, translates "the glorious liberty of the children of God." The Greek text reads: *tēn eleutherian tēs doxēs tōn teknōn tou theou.*

74. Hegel, *Lectures on the Philosophy of Religion,* 1:114, 3:292.

75. Ibid., 3:370. Hegel here uses the traditional language of divine "persons" but regards it to be conceptually inadequate. On Hegel's concept of the Trinity, see Hodgson, *Hegel and Christian Theology,* chap. 6.

76. "Absolute" for Hegel is not a static but a dynamic, relational concept. Absolute Spirit is utterly connected with everything; it is nothing but relationality. The Latin verb *absolvere* (from which "absolute" derives) means to "to loosen from" or "release." This releasing or absolving is what God does in relation to the world. Hodgson, *Hegel and Christian Theology,* 90–91.

77. Hegel, *Lectures on the Philosophy of Religion,* 3:82–83, 192–95, 276, 285–86. On the concept of God as "Spirit" see below, chap. 2, where, too, the discussion of Hegel continues. I do not mean to imply that a radically liberal theology must be a trinitarian theology, although I do believe that the doctrine of the Trinity comes closest to capturing the complex truth about God. After all, the first American liberal theologians were Unitarians. Their problem was that they lacked a dynamic, relational, processive understanding of God, and thus they could not think of God as Hegel did, who found an ingenious way of reconstructing rather than abandoning the classical doctrine of the Trinity. In this

work I am not making claims about how Christian doctrines such as the Trinity and incarnation should be construed. As I have said, liberal theology is a big tent that includes a diversity of views.

78. Hegel, *Lectures on the Philosophy of Religion*, 3:171–73; Hodgson, *Hegel and Christian Theology*, 96–97.

79. These topics are discussed in Hegel's *Elements of the Philosophy of Right* (1820–21), ed. Allen W. Wood, trans. H. B. Nisbet (Cambridge: Cambridge University Press, 1991). In this work, his social ethics, Hegel was unable to resolve a conflict between freedom, equality, and differentiation. Abstract equality produces homogeneity, but differentiation results in gender and social stratifications because Hegel thought of the "articulations" necessary to society along vertical rather than horizontal lines. Such stratifications stand in marked tension with his vision of universal human freedom. See Thomas A. Lewis, *Freedom and Tradition in Hegel: Reconsidering Anthropology, Ethics, and Religion* (Notre Dame: University of Notre Dame Press, 2005), esp. chap. 7.

80. *Lectures on the Philosophy of World History, Introduction: Reason in History*, trans. H. B. Nisbet with an introduction by Duncan Forbes (Cambridge: Cambridge University Press, 1975), 54. This is the place where Hegel distinguishes between Oriental, Greco-Roman, and Christian practices of freedom.

81. Hegel, *Lectures on the Philosophy of Religion*, 2:736–60, 3:359–60. Today Hegel's version of the history of religions must be modified in light of the reality of religious pluralism. See below, chaps. 2, 3.

82. Karl Barth, *Church Dogmatics*, ed. G. W. Bromiley and T. F. Torrance, vol. 2/1 (Edinburgh: T. & T. Clark, 1957), §§ 28–31. When I was a student at Yale Divinity School in the late 1950s, I became an ardent Barthian, absorbing large chunks of the *Church Dogmatics* in courses with Hans Frei, Richard Niebuhr, and Claude Welch. At the same time I was drawn to the nineteenth-century liberal theologians and wrote a dissertation on Ferdinand Christian Baur. Although I have moved toward liberalism and away from Barth, he still has an attraction for me.

83. Ibid., 2/1:313–14.

84. Ibid., 2/1:317, 320. See my discussion of these matters in *Winds of the Spirit*, chap. 11.

85. The seventeenth-century philosopher René Descartes focused everything on the thinking subject: "I think, therefore I am" (*A Discourse on Method,* pt. 4). Hegel in his own way strongly resisted the Cartesian influence in philosophy. This is why Hegel and Barth are bedfellows.

86. Translated as "Liberal Theology: Some Alternatives," in *The Hibbert Journal* 59 (April 1961): 213–19. Timothy Gorringer's essay, "Karl Barth and Liberal Theology," in Chapman, ed., *The Future of Liberal Theology,* 163–69, directed me to this material and offers helpful commentary.

87. On Biedermann, see above, n. 33.

88. Already in his appreciative lectures on Schleiermacher in 1923–24 he considered the possibility that Schleiermacher's theology might be read as a theology of the Holy Spirit. *The Theology of Schleiermacher: Lectures at Göttingen, Winter Semester of 1923/24,* ed. Dietrich Ritschl, trans. G. W. Bromiley (Grand Rapids, Mich.: Wm. B. Eerdmans, 1982), 278–79.

89. Karl Barth, *Evangelical Theology: An Introduction,* trans. Grover Foley (New York: Holt, Rinehart and Winston, 1963), xii. Charles Long remembers Barth saying that this theology would draw upon distinctive aspects of the American experience and advocate a "freedom for humanity," a freedom "to which the Son frees us." Charles Long, "The Black Reality: Toward a Theology of Freedom," *Criterion* 8, no. 1 (1969): 2.

90. My first attempt at articulating a theology of freedom was in a little book called *Children of Freedom: Black Liberation in Christian Perspective* (Philadelphia: Fortress Press, 1974). In the preface (4–5) I quoted these remarks by Barth. Two years later I published *New Birth of Freedom: A Theology of Bondage and Liberation* (Philadelphia: Fortress Press, 1976). The present book is a continuation along the same trajectory.

91. The liberation theologians of Central America have used the phrase *el proyecto de Dios* to indicate what is mean by the *basileia tou theou*. I am indebted to Sharon H. Ringe for this reference.

Chapter 2

1. See Peter C. Hodgson, "The Theological Significance of Hegel Today," chap. 11 in *Hegel and Christian Theology: A Reading of the Lectures on the Philosophy of Religion* (Oxford: Oxford University Press, 2005). This chapter summarizes diverse materials from the *Lectures*. Portions of it found on pp. 259–84 are incorporated into the present chapter and are used by permission of Oxford University Press.

2. See Gary Dorrien's discussion in *The Making of American Liberal Theology*, 3 vols. (Louisville: Westminster John Knox Press, 2001, 2003, 2006), vol. 1: *Imagining Progressive Religion, 1805–1900*, 80ff., 371ff.; vol. 2: *Idealism, Realism, and Modernity, 1900–1950*, 239–41, 286–87, 313ff.; also the index under "Hegel" in vol. 3, *Crisis, Irony, and Postmodernity, 1950–2005*. Royce's *Lectures on Modern Idealism* (New Haven: Yale University Press, 1919) provides a valuable introduction to Hegel's thought.

3. Ferdinand Christian Baur, *On the Writing of Church History*, ed. and trans. Peter C. Hodgson (New York: Oxford University Press, 1968), 276–79, 336–41; and *Lehrbuch der christlichen Dogmengeschichte*, 3rd ed. (Leipzig: Fues's Verlag, 1867), 22–29, 61–62, 95–96, 140–44, 158–60. See Hodgson, *The Formation of Historical Theology: A Study of Ferdinand Christian Baur* (New York: Harper & Row, 1966), chap. 4.

4. Baur, *Lehrbuch der christlichen Dogmengeschichte*, 144–45.

5. My practice is to lowercase the word spirit when it is used in an abstract or philosophical sense and to capitalize it when it refers to God's Spirit, the Holy Spirit.

6. George Hendry, *The Holy Spirit in Christian Theology* (Philadelphia: Westminster Press, 1956), 23; cf. 21–25.

7. Ibid., 37–42.

8. For a fuller discussion of these issues, see Paul Tillich, *Systematic Theology*, 3 vols. (Chicago: University of Chicago Press, 1951–63), 3:148–49; and Peter C. Hodgson, *Winds of the Spirit: A Constructive Christian Theology* (Louisville: Westminster John Knox Press, 1994), 287–91.

9. Hegel called his thinking "speculative" because of its affirmation of a relationship of double mirroring (*speculum* means "mirror") between

consciousness and object. Theologically this means that God is, to be sure, a mirror of consciousness, but consciousness is also a mirror of God, of God's self-knowing in and through human knowledge of God. See Hodgson, *Hegel and Christian Theology*, 7–8, 79–84.

10. Cyril O'Regan, *The Heterodox Hegel* (Albany: State University of New York Press, 1994), 3. This is a brilliant study by a critic of Hegelian heterodoxy.

11. See Hegel's introductions to the *Lectures on the Philosophy of Religion*, 3 vols., ed. and trans. Peter C. Hodgson, et al. (Berkeley and Los Angeles: University of California Press, 1984–87; reprint Oxford: Oxford University Press, 2007), 1:83–184.

12. O'Regan, *The Heterodox Hegel*, 15–20, 251–59, 270–83.

13. Ibid., 300–10.

14. Hodgson, *Hegel and Christian Theology*, 16–17. Gary Dorrien makes the interesting observation that Paul Tillich realized late in life "that 'spirit' was a cleaner and more inclusive category for his theological project than the ontological category of 'being,' but by then . . . it was too late to rethink his system" (*The Making of American Liberal Theology*, 2:516). It is also, I believe (and Dorrien agrees, 3:538–39), a more adequate category than that of "person." If Tillich's system were rethought with the category of spirit, it would be seen to be very close to Hegel's.

15. Emmanuel Levinas, *God, Death, and Time,* trans. Bettina Bergo (Stanford: Stanford University Press, 2000), 121–25; quotation from 124. Martin Heidegger, "The Onto-theo-logical Constitution of Metaphysics," in *Identity and Difference,* trans. Joan Stambaugh (New York: Harper & Row, 1969), 42–74.

16. Levinas, *God, Death, and Time,* 136–39.

17. On Hegel's interpretation of the Trinity and absolute spirit, see *Lectures on the Philosophy of Religion*, 3:77–86, 189–98, 275–90; and Hodgson, *Hegel and Christian Theology*, chap. 6.

18. See Hodgson, *Winds of the Spirit,* 276–87. I draw on these pages in this section.

19. Raimon Panikkar, *The Cosmotheandric Experience* (Maryknoll, N.Y.: Orbis Books, 1993).

20. Karl Barth, *Church Dogmatics,* vol. 2/1, ed. G. W. Bromiley and T. F. Torrance (Edinburgh: T & T Clark, 1957), 285; cf. 284–97 (in a lengthy excursus on the treatment of divine personality in Hegelian theologians and antitheologians of the nineteenth century, Barth does not discuss the fact that for Hegel himself the concept of absolute spirit precisely includes, does not exclude, divine subjectivity and personality). Compare also the views of the founder of Boston personalism, Borden Parker Bownes. Bownes was the most profound and original thinker among late-nineteenth-century American liberal theologians. He absorbed Hegelian ideas through the influence of the Göttingen metaphysician Rudolf Hermann Lotze, with whom he studied. See Dorrien, *The Making of American Liberal Theology,* 1:371–92.

21. Emmanuel Levinas, *Totality and Infinity: An Essay on Exteriority,* trans. Alphonso Lingis (Pittsburgh: Duquesne University Press, 1969), 61–62, 65; *God, Death, and Time,* 146–47.

22. Levinas, *Totality and Infinity,* 50, 102.

23. Hodgson, *Hegel and Christian Theology,* 90–91. On the meaning of "absolute" and "absolving" for Hegel, see above, chap. 1, n. 76.

24. Levinas, *Totality and Infinity,* 74–75, 101, 219. See Robert R. Williams's discussion of this contrast in *Recognition: Fichte and Hegel on the Other* (Albany: State University of New York Press, 1992), 285–86, 297–300.

25. Hegel, *Phenomenology of Spirit,* trans. A. V. Miller (Oxford: Clarendon Press, 1977), 19.

26. Williams, *Recognition,* 267–72. His interpretation is informed by that of G. R. G. Mure, *A Study of Hegel's Logic* (Oxford: Oxford University Press, 1950). On Hegel's triple mediation or triple syllogism, see *Encyclopedia of the Philosophical Sciences,* §§ 183–89 (*The Encyclopaedia Logic,* trans. T. F. Geraets, W. A. Suchting, and H. S. Harris [Indianapolis: Hackett, 1991], 259–64); and Hodgson, *Hegel and Christian Theology,* 9–11, 267–68.

27. *Lectures on the Philosophy of Religion,* 1:374–78, 2:573; Hodgson, *Hegel and Christian Theology,* 104–106.

28. Stephen Crites, *Dialectic and Gospel in the Development of Hegel's Thinking* (University Park, Pa.: Pennsylvania State University Press, 1998), 517–26.

29. *Encyclopedia of the Philosophical Sciences,* § 573 (see *G. W. F. Hegel: Theologian of the Spirit,* ed. Peter C. Hodgson [Minneapolis: Fortress Press, 1997], 150–51); *Lectures on the Philosophy of Religion,* 1:379–80; Hodgson, *Hegel and Christian Theology,* 35, 44–45, 80.

30. This is the view of Jacques Derrida and Michel Foucault. Both thinkers reject a sociopolitical as well as a religious holism and thus find no possibility of achieving justice through a social process or redemption through a religious process. The only hope, if any, lies beyond politics and religion in an apocalyptic negation/gift. See Anselm Kyonsuk Min's discussion and critique in *The Solidarity of Others in a Divided World: A Postmodern Theology after Postmodernism* (New York: T & T Clark International, 2004).

31. See Paul Ricoeur, *Time and Narrative,* 3 vols., trans. Kathleen Blamey and David Pellauer (Chicago: University of Chicago Press, 1984–88), esp. vol. 3, chaps. 4–8.

32. O'Regan, *The Heterodox Hegel,* esp. chap. 7. On Hegel and narrative, see Ricoeur, "Should We Renounce Hegel?" chap. 9 in *Time and Narrative,* vol. 3.

33. Williams, *Recognition,* 228, cf. 231–40.

34. *Phenomenology of Spirit,* 10.

35. *Lectures on the Philosophy of Religion,* 3:92–108, 201–11, 295–310.

36. The tragic condition of the world is reflected back into the divine life in the sense that, by envisioning the creation of a finite material world as God's external other, God also envisions the prospect of fall and evil as necessary or inevitable by-products of creation. According to Hegel, this inwardizing of the tragic in God is the function of the mythological figure of Lucifer, the firstborn, fallen Son (ibid., 3:200, 292). Then the second, good Son, Christ, suffers the consequences of worldly evil, and God dies on the cross. In this double sense Hegel offers a radical doctrine of evil.

37. *Phenomenology of Spirit,* 453.

38. *Lectures on the Philosophy of Religion,* 3:158–60.

39. Ibid., 3:336.

40. For Hegel's christology, see *Lectures on the Philosophy of Religion*, 3:109–33, 211–23, 310–28.

41. Ibid., 3:215.

42. Hegel's most explicit statement to this effect is as follows: "Christ speaks not merely as a teacher, who expounds on the basis of his own subjective insight and who is aware of what he is saying and doing, but rather as a prophet. He is the one who, because his demand is immediate, expresses it immediately from God, and God speaks it through him. His having this life of the Spirit in the truth, so that it is simply there without mediation, expresses itself prophetically in such a way that it is God who says it. It is a matter of the absolute, divine truth that has being in and for itself, and of its expression and intention; and the confirmation of this expression is envisaged as God's doing. It is the consciousness of the real unity of the divine will and of his harmony with it. In the form of this expression, however, the accent is laid upon the fact that the one who says this is at the same time essentially human. It is the son of humanity who speaks thus, in whom this expression, this activity of what subsists in and for itself, is essentially the work of God—not as something suprahuman that appears in the shape of an external revelation, but rather as [God's] working in a human being, so that the divine presence is essentially identical with this human being." Ibid., 3:320.

43. H. Richard Niebuhr, *Christ and Culture* (New York: Harper & Brothers, 1951). In the first chapter Niebuhr sets forth his typology of five ways of relating Christ and culture.

44. Ibid., chap. 2.

45. Ibid., chap. 3.

46. In later writings, as I have indicated in chapter 1, Niebuhr modified his critique of liberalism. He also modified the christocentrism of *Christ and Culture*, preferring subsequently to speak of "radical monotheism," and he was critical of the "christism" that characterizes much of Protestant piety. See *The Purpose of the Church and Its Ministry*, in collaboration with Daniel Day Williams and James M. Gustafson (New York: Harper and Brothers, 1956), 44–46; and *Radical Monotheism and Western Culture* (New York: Harper & Brothers, 1960).

47. Niebuhr, *Christ and Culture,* chap. 4.

48. Ibid., chap. 5.

49. Ibid., chap. 6.

50. Ibid., 195–96. The imagery of lifting up and drawing comes from the Gospel of John (12:32), and indeed, according to Niebuhr, the conversion/transformation motif is most clearly evident in the Johannine literature.

51. Hegelian and Kierkegaardian motifs echo here: Hegel describes religion as the elevation of humanity to God, an elevation accomplished for the Christian religion by God's descent into humanity (*Lectures on the Philosophy of Religion,* 1:207–08, 259, 414–15, 419), and Kierkegaard names Christ the Inviter and the Helper who from on high draws all to himself (*Practice in Christianity,* ed. and trans. Howard V. and Edna H. Hong [Princeton: Princeton University Press, 1991], 11ff., 151ff.).

52. Niebuhr, *Christ and Culture,* 215–16.

53. Ibid., 225.

54. Hick describes this process as "a transformation of human existence from self-centredness to a recentring in what in our inadequate human terms we speak of as God, or as Ultimate Reality, or the Transcendent, or the Real." John Hick, *A Christian Theology of Religions: The Rainbow of Faiths* (Louisville: Westminster John Knox Press, 1995), 18.

55. See above, n. 46.

56. Niebuhr, *Christ and Culture,* 11–29. In contrast to the orthodox two-natures christology, Niebuhr's christology bears many of the marks of Protestant liberalism.

57. Paul Rasor, *Faith without Certainty: Liberal Theology in the 21st Century* (Boston: Skinner House Books, 2005), 22–24.

58. Ibid., 86–102.

59. *Lectures on the Philosophy of Religion,* 3:133–42.

60. Williams, *Recognition,* chaps. 7, 9.

61. *Lectures on the Philosophy of Religion,* 3:158–62, 237–47, 339–47.

62. He does in other writings, such as the *Elements of the Philosophy of Right* (ed. Allen W. Wood, trans. H. B. Nisbet [Cambridge: Cambridge University Press, 1991]), where among other things he considers problems

of poverty, division of labor, family relations, and political representation. The extent to which Hegel's philosophical theology is and is not socially transformative is discussed by Andrew Shanks in *Hegel's Political Theology* (Cambridge: Cambridge: University Press, 1991), and *God and Modernity: A New and Better Way to Do Theology* (London and New York: Routledge, 2000). Shanks points out that for Hegel the secular state and its universities represented a liberation from the authority of the church, which dominated European politics and education for centuries. Today the situation is quite different, and Shanks suggests that Hegel would no longer set forth a "grand narrative" as the basis of a university education designed to challenge a hegemonic church but would rather embrace various social movements that are struggling for freedom against a hegemonic state.

63. Diana L. Eck, *A New Religious America* (San Francisco: HarperSanFrancisco, 2001), 69.

64. Hegel and Beethoven were born in the same year, 1770, and it is not implausible to suggest that Hegel became the Beethoven of philosophy and Beethoven the Hegel of music: they both sought pattern, harmony, and redemption in and through a world of conflict, disharmony, and suffering. Beethoven died in 1827, Hegel in 1831.

65. With the exception of Ernst Troeltsch, only the most recent generation of liberal theologians has seriously engaged the challenge of religious pluralism.

66. Hodgson, *Hegel and Christian Theology,* chap. 10.

67. Ibid., 239–43.

68. See Hegel's *Philosophy of Nature,* Part Two of the *Encyclopaedia of the Philosophical Sciences,* trans. A. V. Miller (Oxford: Clarendon Press, 1970), §§ 246–47 (esp. 7–8, 13); Stephen Houlgate, ed., *Hegel and the Philosophy of Nature* (Albany: State University of New York Press, 1998); and Alison Stone, *Petrified Intelligence: Nature in Hegel's Philosophy* (Albany: State University of New York Press, 2004), who, in addition to analyzing the logic of Hegel's philosophy of nature, assesses its relevance to environmental issues.

69. The recent work of Philip Clayton holds promise of providing such a basis. He combines resources from Hegel and Whitehead with a knowl-

edge of quantum physics and the brain sciences: *God and Contemporary Science* (Edinburgh: Edinburgh University Press, 1996), and *Mind and Emergence: From Quantum to Consciousness* (Oxford: Oxford University Press, 2004). See Gary Dorrien's discussion of Clayton in *The Making of American Liberal Theology,* 3:535–37.

Chapter 3

1. In this chapter I make use of materials from my book *Winds of the Spirit: A Constructive Christian Theology* (Louisville: Westminster John Knox Press, 1994), chaps. 6–8, 13, 18. Used by permission of the publisher. The most recent publication of the Workgroup on Constructive Christian Theology, *Constructive Theology: A Contemporary Approach to Classical Themes,* ed. Serene Jones and Paul Lakeland (Minneapolis: Fortress Press, 2005), introduces a new generation of liberal/postliberal theologians and advances the discussion of these and other issues from a great diversity of perspectives.

2. Hodgson, *Winds of the Spirit,* chap. 14.

3. See Gary Dorrien's discussion of Henry Ward Beecher, Elizabeth Cady Stanton, Washington Gladden, Walter Rauschenbusch, and Vida Scudder in *The Making of American Liberal Theology* (Louisville: Westminster John Knox Press, 2001, 2003), vol. 1: *Imagining Progressive Religion,* chaps. 4–5; vol. 2: *Idealism, Realism, and Modernity,* chap. 2. Rauschenbusch, who had an enormous impact, made the imagery of the kingdom of God central to a theology of the social gospel, but he was not sensitive to issues of race and was conflicted about the rights of women. Scudder was a more radical thinker than Rauschenbusch, radical in both her politics and her Anglo-Catholic socialist Christian vision.

4. Gustavo Gutiérrez, *A Theology of Liberation: History, Politics, and Salvation,* 15th anniversary edition, trans. and ed. Caridad Inda and John Eagleson (Maryknoll, N.Y.: Orbis Books, 1988); *The Power of the Poor in History,* trans. Robert R. Barr (Maryknoll, N.Y.: Orbis Books, 1983); *The Truth Shall Make You Free: Confrontations,* trans. Matthew J. O'Connell (Maryknoll, N.Y.: Orbis Books, 1990); *The God of Life,*

trans. Robert R. Barr (Maryknoll, N.Y.: Orbis Books, 1991). Other important contributors to Latin American and Hispanic liberation theologies are Leonardo and Clodovis Boff, José Comblin, Enrique Dussel, José Míquez Bonino, Juan Luis Segundo, Jon Sobrino, Sergio Torres, Ada María Isasi-Díaz. The emerging voices of African theology are part of the future of liberation theology.

5. Gutiérrez, *The Truth Shall Make You Free*, 7–11, 55–57.

6. See above, pp. 21–22.

7. Aloysius Pieris, *An Asian Theology of Liberation* (Maryknoll, N.Y.: Orbis Books, 1988); *Love Meets Wisdom: A Christian Experience of Buddhism* (Maryknoll, N.Y.: Orbis Books, 1988). Other important Asian theologies are the Korean Minjung and the writings of Asian women; see works by C. S. Song, David Kwang-sun Suh, Virginia Fabella, Sun Ai Le Park, Chung Hyun Kyung, Kwok Pui-Lan.

8. Aloysius Pieris, "The Buddha and the Christ: Mediators of Liberation," in *The Myth of Christian Uniqueness: Toward a Pluralistic Theology of Religions*, ed. John Hick and Paul F. Knitter (Maryknoll, N.Y.: Orbis Books, 1987), 175.

9. James H. Cone, *Black Theology and Black Power* (New York: Seabury Press, 1969); *A Black Theology of Liberation* (Philadelphia: Lippincott, 1970); *The Spirituals and the Blues* (New York: Seabury Press, 1972); *God of the Oppressed* (New York: Seabury Press, 1975); *Black Theology: A Documentary History, 1966–1979* (edited with Gayraud Wilmore; Maryknoll, N.Y.: Orbis Books, 1979). See also the contributions of James Evans, Deotis Roberts, Gayraud Wilmore, Cornel West, Dwight Hopkins, Katie Cannon, Jacquelyn Grant, Delores Williams, Shawn Copeland, Emilie Townes, and Barbara Holmes. An earlier generation of black theologians, notably Benjamin Mays and Howard Thurman, was very much shaped in the liberal tradition. Martin Luther King Jr. was a student of the last generation of personalists, and at Boston University he was influenced by Thurman. On the impact of Reinhold Niebuhr's *Moral Man and Immoral Society* (New York: Scribner's, 1932), his most brilliant work of social criticism, see Dorrien, *The Making of American Liberal Theology*, 2:449-51. Among other topics, Niebuhr discussed civil disobedience and nonviolent resistance, and predicted that one day these strategies would be used by American blacks in their struggle for racial justice (Niebuhr, 252-54).

10. Cone, *Black Theology and Black Power,* 26–28. In later writings Cone modifies his use of the rhetoric of black power. I return to this issue below.

11. William R. Jones, *Is God a White Racist? A Preamble to Black Theology* (Garden City, N.Y.: Doubleday, 1973).

12. This is one of Ernst Troeltsch's deepest insights. See "The Ethics of Cultural Values," in *Christian Thought: Its History and Application,* ed. Baron F. von Hügel (London: University of London Press, 1923), 69–99. From Troeltsch we learn that such conclusions are congruent with theological liberalism at its best, countering the cultural optimism and evolutionary progressivism that characterized many of its late nineteenth- and early twentieth-century adherents. He distinguishes between the compromise of capitulation and the compromise that creates what is possible in a given circumstance.

13. Rosemary Radford Ruether, *Sexism and God-Talk: Toward a Feminist Theology,* with a new introduction (Boston: Beacon Press, 1993); *Gaia and God: An Ecofeminist Theology of Earth Healing* (San Francisco: HarperSanFrancisco, 1992); *Women-Church: Theology and Practice of Feminist Liturgical Communities* (San Francisco: Harper & Row, 1985). See also the important work of Elizabeth Johnson, Elisabeth Schüssler Fiorenza, Sallie McFague, Catherine Keller, Sharon Welch, Mary McClintock Fulkerson, Serene Jones, and many others. Present-day feminist theology has its roots in the abolitionist and suffragist struggles of the nineteenth and early twentieth centuries. A twentieth-century pioneer was one of Ruether's predecessors at Garrett Seminary, Georgia Harkness, who was a student of Edgar Brightman.

14. Mark Lewis Taylor, *Religion, Politics, and the Christian Right: Post–9/11 Powers and American Empire* (Minneapolis: Fortress Press, 2005), 129–41.

15. See the evidence adduced by Taylor (n. 14); by Gary Dorrien, *Imperial Designs: Neoconservatism and the New Pax Americana* (New York: Routledge, 2004); and by David Ray Griffin, John B. Cobb, Jr., and Catherine Keller, *The American Empire and the Commonwealth of God* (Louisville: Westminster John Knox Press, 2006). I discuss these matters in "Christian Theology in an Age of Terror," *Witherspoon Network*

News 25, no. 1 (Winter 2005): 4–7; and 25, no. 2 (Spring 2005): 5–8. Support for this analysis comes from a surprising source: Kevin Phillips, *American Theocracy: The Peril and Politics of Radical Religion, Oil, and Borrowed Money in the 21st Century* (New York: Viking, 2006). Phillips shows how a ruthless imperial politics has been molded from an alliance between the economy of oil, theocratic religion, and the "financialization" of the United States. I take issue with his use of the adjective *radical* to describe the religion involved, which is a militant form of fundamentalism that has utterly distorted the true *radix* of religion.

16. Harold Pinter, "Art, Truth and Politics," text of 2005 Nobel Prize lecture, *The Guardian,* 7 Dec. 2005.

17. Paul Rasor, *Faith without Certainty: Liberal Theology in the 21st Century* (Boston: Skinner House Books, 2005), 141–63.

18. Cone, *God of the Oppressed,* 10, 39–52.

19. Friedrich Schleiermacher, *On Religion: Speeches to Its Cultured Despisers,* ed. and trans. Richard Crouter (Cambridge: Cambridge University Press, 1988).

20. Rasor, quoting Eduardo Mendieta, in *Faith without Certainty,* 145.

21. See the reference to Gutiérrez above, n. 5.

22. Peter Beinart argues to this effect in *The Good Fight: Why Liberals—and Only Liberals—Can Win the War on Terror and Make America Great Again* (New York: HarperCollins, 2006). See the summary of his argument in "The Rehabilitation of the Cold-War Liberal," *The New York Times Magazine,* April 30, 2006, 41–45.

23. I am thinking of the work of Ian Barbour, Paul Davies, Arthur Peacocke, John Polkinghorne, Ted Peters, Brian Swimme, Gordon Kaufman, Catherine Keller, Philip Clayton, and others. See Barbour, *Religion in an Age of Science* (San Francisco: Harper & Row, 1990); Davies, *God and the New Physics* (New York: Simon & Schuster, 1983), and *The Cosmic Blueprint* (New York: Simon & Schuster, 1988); Peacocke, *Creation and the World of Science* (Oxford: Clarendon Press, 1979), and *Theology for a Scientific Age* (Oxford: Basil Blackwell, 1990); Polkinghorne, *One World: The Interaction of Science and Theology* (Princeton: Princeton University Press, 1983), and *Science and Providence: God's Interaction with the World* (Boston: Shambhala Publications, 1989); Peters, ed., *Cosmos as Creation:*

Theology and Science in Consonance (Nashville: Abingdon Press, 1989); Swimme, *The Universe Is a Green Dragon: A Cosmic Creation Story* (Santa Fe: Bear & Co., 1984); Kaufman, *In Face of Mystery: A Constructive Theology* (Cambridge, Mass.: Harvard University Press, 1993); Keller, *Face of the Deep: A Theology of Becoming* (London and New York: Routledge, 2003); Clayton, *Mind and Emergence: From Quantum to Consciousness* (Oxford: Oxford University Press, 2004).

24. Sallie McFague, *The Body of God: An Ecological Theology* (Minneapolis: Fortress Press, 1993), 56–57. She is following a suggestion of Stephen Toulmin, *The Return to Cosmology: Postmodern Science and the Theology of Nature* (Berkeley and Los Angeles: University of California Press, 1982), 272.

25. Thomas Berry, *The Dream of the Earth* (San Francisco: Sierra Club Books, 1988), 37–39, 41–42.

26. Charles Birch and John B. Cobb, Jr., *The Liberation of Life: From the Cell to the Community* (Cambridge: Cambridge University Press, 1981), esp. 79–96.

27. A term suggested by Birch and Cobb. I draw on their work in the following paragraphs.

28. This is an idea that Robert C. Calhoun, one of the most brilliant of the old Yale liberals, introduced into his lectures on systematic theology. He said something like this (from my lecture notes, Yale Divinity School, spring 1958): The world was created with a principle of indeterminacy and waywardness, so that humans could have an environment in which freedom is genuinely possible. The world did not consciously rebel against the ground of its being; no consciousness and will are found in the natural creation. But the world in its waywardness falls into evil to the extent that in disorder it ceases to function as it was created to function. The disorder takes the form of encroachment and destruction. Mosquitoes are good— except when they are unduly encroaching on other creatures. God does not eliminate the waywardness and indeterminacy of the world. Rather, God redeems the world, restores it, by constantly acting so as to produce order, direction, and purpose. God does not eliminate the indeterminate backdrop against which human freedom is possible. Rather, God keeps the backdrop from getting out of hand. Thus, God does not eliminate

mosquitoes but enables humans to control malaria. The world is "good" insofar as it *is,* but "evil" insofar as in its waywardness it has fallen into encroachment, destruction, and disorder.

29. Stuart Kaufmann, *At Home in the Universe: The Search for Laws of Self-Organization and Complexity* (New York: Oxford University Press, 1994). I think we have to add that from a theological perspective the universe is not our *final* home; that is what God is.

30. The story in Genesis 6–9 depicts a change in God's attitude from a determination to drown out evil to a promise never again to destroy all flesh by a flood. But the change is really in the human perception of God.

31. Romans 8:20-21. See above, p. 23.

32. Hyo-Dong Lee, *Spirit and Dao: Two Politico-Ecological Dialectics of Freedom in Hegel and Laozi,* Ph.D. Dissertation, Vanderbilt University, 2005. The ideas mentioned in this paragraph come from correspondence with the author. Lee suggests that the two dialectics represent complementary variations on the logic of freedom as self-presence and other-presence. With Hegel the balance is tilted to the reconciling/stabilizing force of self-identity, while with Daoism it is tilted to the disruptive/centrifugal play of difference. My version of ecological theology reflects the Hegelian tilt although it seeks a truer balance.

33. The seminal work in recounting the move in Christian theology to religious pluralism is John Hick and Paul F. Knitter, eds., *The Myth of Christian Uniqueness: Toward a Pluralistic Theology of Religions* (Mary-knoll, N.Y.: Orbis Books, 1987). The discussion is extended to a multifaith perspective in Paul F. Knitter, ed., *The Myth of Religious Superiority: A Multifaith Exploration* (Maryknoll, N.Y.: Orbis Books, 2005).

34. John Hick has consistently held this view. See *The Myth of Christian Uniqueness,* 16–36; and *The Myth of Religious Superiority,* 3–12.

35. John B. Cobb Jr. argues for such a position in Gavin D'Costa, ed., *Christian Uniqueness Reconsidered: The Myth of a Pluralistic Theology of Religion* (Maryknoll, N.Y.: Orbis Books, 1990), 81–95. Most of the contributors to this volume oppose religious pluralism on the grounds that Christianity loses its distinctive identity if it surrenders its claim to absolute and superior truth; but Cobb argues for a more radical pluralism.

36. Paul F. Knitter discusses the views of S. Mark Heim, James L. Fredericks, and Francis X. Clooney in *Introducing Theologies of Religions* (Maryknoll, N.Y.: Orbis Books, 2002), chap. 11.

37. Ibid., chap. 12.

38. Hyo-Dong Lee, "Interreligious Dialogue as a Politics of Recognition: A Postcolonial Rereading of Hegel for Interreligious Solidarity," *The Journal of Religion* 85 (Oct. 2005): 555–81.

39. "The Spirit and Religious Pluralism," *The Myth of Religious Superiority*, ed. Knitter, 135–50. A slightly different version of the essay appears in *Horizons* 31 (Spring 2004): 22–39. Materials from this article are incorporated into the following paragraphs. Used by permission of Orbis Books. I have been especially influenced by the work of Ernst Troeltsch, Paul Tillich, Karl Rahner, and Raimundo Panikkar. See Troeltsch, "The Place of Christianity among the World-Religions" and "Ethics and the Philosophy of History," in *Christian Thought: Its History and Application*, 1–129; Tillich, "The Significance of the History of Religions for the Systematic Theologian," in *The Future of Religions*, ed. Jerald C. Brauer (New York: Harper & Row, 1966), 80–94; Rahner, "Experience of the Holy Spirit," in *Theological Investigations*, vol. 18, trans. Edward Quinn (New York: Crossroad, 1983), 189–210; and Panikkar, "The Jordan, the Tiber, and the Ganges: Three Kairological Moments of Christic Self-Consciousness," in *The Myth of Christian Uniqueness*, ed. Hick and Knitter, 89–116.

40. An expression used by Tillich in *The Future of Religions*, 87–88. On the Trinity, see above, pp. 24, 39–40.

41. Principally John L. Esposito, Darrell J. Fasching, and Todd Lewis, *World Religions Today* (Oxford: Oxford University Press, 2002), chaps. 5–6. I have also made use of a few books that focus on Hindu-Christian and Buddhist-Christian dialogue: Francis X. Clooney, S.J., *Hindu Wisdom for All God's Children* (Maryknoll, N.Y.: Orbis Books, 1998); Rita M. Gross and Terry C. Muck, eds., *Buddhists Talk about Jesus, Christians Talk about the Buddha* (New York: Continuum, 2000); John B. Cobb, Jr., *Beyond Dialogue: Toward a Mutual Transformation of Christianity and Buddhism* (Philadelphia: Fortress Press, 1982); John B. Cobb, Jr., and Christopher Ives, eds., *The Emptying God: A Buddhist-Jewish-Christian*

Conversation (Maryknoll, N.Y.: Orbis Books, 1990); Aloysius Pieris, *Love Meets Wisdom: A Christian Experience of Buddhism* (Maryknoll, N.Y.: Orbis Books, 1988); and Paula M. Cooey, William R. Eakin, and Jay B. McDaniel, eds., *After Patriarchy: Feminist Transformations of the World Religions* (Maryknoll, N.Y.: Orbis Books, 1991). This comparative study should be extended to include Judaism, Islam, East Asian religions, the religions of indigenous peoples—a challenge that exceeds my capacity. With Islam the challenge is especially difficult but all the more urgent.

42. This expression is suggested by the title of S. Mark Heim's book, *The Depth of Riches: A Trinitarian Theology of Religions* (Grand Rapids, Mich.: Wm. B. Eerdmans, 2001). My point of view and argument, however, are quite different from Heim's.

43. Esposito, Fasching, and Lewis, *World Religions Today,* 282.

44. Ibid., 361–64, 371–73.

45. Cobb, *Beyond Dialogue,* chaps. 4–5.

46. In Cobb and Ives, eds., *The Emptying God,* 3–65.

47. This is clearly the position of José Ignacio Cabezón and Rita M. Gross in *Buddhists Talk about Jesus, Christians Talk about the Buddha.* See also the essay by Bonnie Thurston, who is critical of this position from a Christian perspective.

48. Taitetsu Unno, "Contrasting Images of the Buddha," in *Buddhists Talk about Jesus, Christians Talk about the Buddha,* 140–42. I have substituted the Sanskrit for the Pali spelling—*dharma* rather than *dhamma*—in this quotation.

49. Ibid., 142.

50. For a good discussion of these aspects, more from a postliberal than a liberal perspective, see David H. Kelsey, *Imagining Redemption* (Louisville: Westminster John Knox Press, 2005).

51. I am haunted by the cynical slogan inscribed above the gate to Auschwitz, *Arbeit macht frei*—"work brings freedom." This slogan greeted arriving prisoners as well as those who returned to the camp after forced labor at nearby factories. The work of Auschwitz was not the work of God but of the devil, of the demonic in history, and what it brought is not freedom

but a concentration unto death organized with a terrifying rationality. The slogan is said to have been devised by the camp commandant, Rudolf Hoess, who believed that self-sacrifice in the form of brutal, death-inducing labor leads to a kind of spiritual freedom. His was a demonically distorted, nihilistic spirituality, and Auschwitz has become the principal symbol of the depravity of which the human spirit is capable. What is highest in humanity—rationality and freedom—is here converted into what is lowest. This possibility must be faced by liberal theology. Auschwitz represents an interruption of theological claims and renders them ever unfinished. See Otto Friedrich, *The Kingdom of Auschwitz* (New York: HarperPerennial, 1994), 2–4; and Laurence Rees, *Auschwitz: A New History* (New York: PublicAffairs, 2005), chap. 1.

52. Historian Fritz Stern's memoir, *Five Germanys I Have Known* (New York: Farrar, Straus and Giroux, 2006), points to this danger. Stern, who emigrated to the United States with his parents in 1938 to escape Nazi persecution, notes that in Germany attacks on liberalism began before the First World War, intensified during the Weimar Republic, and reached their culmination in National Socialism. He then writes, in reference to the United States, "I have become ever more concerned that this country's generous liberal spirit, itself ever in need of renewal and correction, has in the last half century been under attack. I opposed the radical detractors of liberalism in the 1960s, and since then I have watched pseudo-conservatives and fundamentalists undermine the nation's celebrated commitment to reason and tolerance" (10; cf. 226–28, 249–61, 451–54). One of the questions raised by this book is whether something similar to what happened in Germany could happen here.

Index